Dan Cox is there in some of my earliest memories. I wrestled him in the basement of his uncle's house. We waterskiied together nearly every week in the summers. Dan and his wife, Cheryl, went to Afghanistan with my wife, Marti, and me in 1971, and about ten years later I steered the process to install Dan as the pastor of the small church that he eventually developed into a megachurch. I was very proud of him—and worried. Marti and I saw the pain between Dan and Cheryl; we saw evidence of that pain in their kids. We prayed for them, as we saw the pressure and growing disconnect between their private and public lives, and we grieved with them as the pain became unbearable.

In the story of the Prodigal Son, we read of the joyous homecoming when the father's love easily eclipses all demands for punishment. But we don't get any glimpse into the inevitable process of unraveling—the complicated consequences of the son's unreasonable demands and loss of half of his father's estate. Dan's story offers such a glimpse. The all-encompassing love of the Father is easily greater than Dan's failings, though there are undoubtedly those who cannot accept that his is simply forgiven. Now secure that he has the Father's love and acceptance, Dan continues to unravel the complex, painful knots of faith, of trauma, and of consequence.

LYNN GREEN, FORMER INTERNATIONAL CHAIRMAN OF YOUTH WITH A MISSION

In *Disillusioned,* Dan Cox rigorously scrutinizes his beliefs and relates his failings, all with the hope of discovering the truth. His book will provide encouragement to those who are discouraged with the narrowness of their church, whether pastors or parishioners. It's apparent Dan has become a much better servant of Christ through his brokenness.

PAUL BEEN, LICENSED PROFESSIONAL COUNSELOR (RETIRED)
DENVER SEMINARY HOSPICE CHAPLAIN

Some Christians may find Dan Cox's crisis of faith disturbing. But disillusionment is a fact of life, and *Disillusioned* forces us to deal with that reality. In ministry it is tempting to project an unrealistic image of our faith and our personal life. But eventually it catches up with us, as it did with Dan. While I do not agree with all of his conclusions, we can all identify with the challenging journey of faith and doubt he presents. Dan goes into the underbelly of life in ministry, and with brutal honesty he confronts his sin, his failures, and the possibility of redemption.

RICK OLMSTEAD, PASTOR OF VINEYARD CHURCH OF THE ROCKIES, FORT COLLINS, CO

It is rare to look through a window into a person's dark-night-of-the-soul experience, but that's what this book is. Dan Cox's spiritual crisis might have felt like "God left the building and turned the lights off on his way out." This book is written for those who identify with Dan's journey. Prepare for brutal personal honesty, self-examination, acceptance of responsibility, and an emotional ebb and flow as you read deeper. There will be something that strikes your heart.

GARY STEPHENS, INTERNATIONALLY RECOGNIZED HUMANITARIAN; AUTHOR,
WAITING FOR A FATHER: HEARING THE HEART-CRY OF THE ORPHANS OF THE WORLD

Sometimes we Christians, when faced with insurmountable odds, seem to embrace the infamous fatalistic demeanor of "The Charge Of The Light Brigade" as we faithfully declare, "Ours is not to question why, ours is but to do and die." But why not question God or wonder why? Why do we think we must keep it all in, as if God cannot handle our questions? Sometimes the challenges of life leave us feeling like sheep surrounded by wolves, and it can feel like our Good Shepherd is missing in action. King David questioned God, as did Job.

Dan Cox hit that proverbial wall and has written the book that few would write, giving us deep insight into his journey from disillusionment to new-found faith and grace. The words of experience written here were given to us through blood and tears—both Dan's and God's.

Here we find that even though all in life is shakable, God is unshakable in His love for us. A remarkable work, which can help us understand the depths of disillusionment and the pathway back.

JEFFREY CRAIG FENHOLT, CONTEMPORARY CHRISTIAN RECORDING ARTIST
APPEARED ON THE COVER OF *TIME MAGAZINE* IN 1971, AS THE ORIGINAL "JESUS"
IN THE BROADWAY ADAPTATION OF "JESUS CHRIST SUPERSTAR."

A dynamic journey from doctrine to disillusionment, to despair, to discovery, to direction.

ANN BEEN

To Sally
May faith be Yours!
I hope you find
enlightenment Encouragement
and understanding about Your
cousin   Best Wishes
Dan.

Disillusioned

A Journey from Certainty to Faith

DISILLUSIONED

A Journey from Certainty to Faith

Dan Cox

with Carmen Radley

DISILLUSIONED
A JOURNEY FROM CERTAINTY TO FAITH
© 2014 by Dan Cox with Carmen Radley

Deep River Books
Sisters, Oregon
www.deepriverbooks.com

ISBN – 13: 9781940269085
ISBN – 10: 1940269083

Library of Congress: 2013954736

Printed in the USA

Cover design by Joe Bailen, Contajus Designs

For Wendy, Mary, and Jon.

These are not, however, the days of miracles, and I suppose it will be granted that I am not to expect a direct revelation. I must study the plain physical facts of the case, ascertain what is possible and learn what appears to be wise and right.

ABRAHAM LINCOLN,

(on whether to wait on revelation from God
to issue the Emancipation Proclamation)

Contents

PREFACE

Conventional, comforting Christianity has failed. It does not work.
For the churches that insist on preaching it, the jig is up.

DIANA BUTLER BASS, *CHRISTIANITY AFTER RELIGION*

I have become a statistic.

Only six years ago, I was the pastor of an evangelical megachurch of several thousand people. A churchgoer since birth, I had committed my entire life to spreading the gospel. Now, I can't get myself through the doors of a church. I can hardly lift my voice in prayer.

I'm a statistic: I'm just one of a growing number of people disillusioned with contemporary Christianity. One report shows that each year, around 2.7 million of us fall away. In what historian Diana Butler Bass calls "the Great Religious Recession," we are walking away in droves, a disenchanted chorus echoing a sad refrain: "This just didn't work for me." From my experience and from speaking with so many others, I know the recently "dechurched" are confused, hurt, angry, and afraid. We've lost the framework for making sense of our precarious human condition. Swelling the ranks of those identifying as "spiritual but not religious," a group comprising 30 percent of American adults, we're searching for where to go next. We still long for the Divine, but we haven't found him where we were told to look.

For me, this disillusionment was a startling reality. I've been a Christian since the cradle and was taught that there was no other way but the narrow path offered by my fundamentalist church. In 1970, I joined Youth With A Mission and traveled to Afghanistan. Armed with youthful enthusiasm and a real passion for the Word of God, I hoped to share a message that would soothe and comfort members of my generation who were disillusioned by consumerist, workaday America and were seeking enlightenment in the East, exploring drugs and counterculture and anything they could to find meaning in their lives. Of course, we believed the message of Christ would bring just that meaning, and in some cases, it did.

After this experience, I returned to the United States wanting to open doors for the unchurched, for those who hadn't grown up with the rules, regulations, and rituals of traditional Christianity and who were uncomfortable in those spaces. I began preaching in the early 1980s, and by 2006, my congregation was nearly two hundred times the size of the modest little church we started with.

But even though it all seemed so steady, so certain, so sure, the structure did not hold. I was overloaded and overwhelmed. My responsibilities as pastor were too much, and my family life was worse. I was facing doubt on so many issues—about who God was, about prayer, marriage, the church organization, my own humanity, my career—and I was flooded with anxiety and depression. Despite my belief that it couldn't, everything I knew fell apart.

I have spent a long time figuring out what led me to this place, and even longer climbing my way back to a place where I can live—where I can accept who I am and be comfortable with what I believe. Much of my story is told in the following pages. The strange thing is, I have always wanted to write a book to help people, to share a message that would inspire them on their journeys, but I believed it would be because I had gotten everything right and I had all the answers.

Instead, I'm sharing my failures.

Instead, I have more questions than ever before.

With those things in mind, I will need your mercy as I tell my story. In this book, I speak honestly and openly about some of the greatest mistakes of my life with the hope that sharing the whole journey will be salve for a wound or relief for someone who is struggling. The biggest mistake I will share with you is an extramarital affair I had just after I resigned my position as senior pastor at the church. I transgressed in a nearly unspeakable way, I hurt many of the people I love the most, and I have paid dearly for my transgression.

But I have also learned so much through the mistakes I have made. I have been able to rid myself of all that is not essential on my spiritual journey. Instead, there are two things I cling to: that there is a God, and Jesus is his Son. Everything else I take one step at a time.

Many of you may be in the same place, and you know that this process is incredibly confusing and, frankly, terrifying. You are cutting yourself free from the moorings of everything that you have ever known. You don't know what to believe or trust. You feel like a ship moving away from a coastline that you'll never see again.

For many people raised in church, abandoning that coastline—that well-defined, safe, steady place—is so terrifying that when you sail out on that ship, the open sea is shocking compared to the security of staying in the quiet, closed-off harbor.

In my own life, it was like I believed that the earth was flat, and that if I moved too far from the coast, I'd fall off the edge into oblivion. Recently, I came across this telling adage that sums up my life: "Ships are the safest in the harbors, but they weren't built to stay there." I think that is true in our quest with God. It's safe to be in those places where everything is familiar and predictable, but when your faith is not meeting you, you have to cut away and find what is going to help you grow in your journey with God.

Of course, it isn't easy. Even now, many years after I left that coast, I wake up in the middle of the night, afraid of what it means that I've taken such a path, that I've moved so far away from what I once thought was true. I wake up afraid that people will read this book and condemn me. I worry that I'll be misunderstood. I worry that this tense, messy process will fall on deaf ears.

After all, I am baring my soul in these pages.

But I can't keep from telling my story. Because I truly believe that if we do not confront the problems we face in our churches—whether the hypocrisy we see, the judgment we detest, the contradictions we note between how the church functions and what Jesus taught, or even the fact that we are bored out of our minds from hearing the same sermons over and over again, bored senseless with the trite platitudes and easy clichés that we tell each other each time we don't have the answer—then we are just delaying the inevitable.

Ultimately, the veil will fall away from our eyes, and we will see where we were not being authentic. We will see where we were conforming to an organization or to someone else's thinking. We will see where we squelched our questions and turned off our minds and deferred to someone else out of fear of the unknown.

So I hope my story is a place for us to meet and explore an open and dynamic faith. This place is where we can join together, a safe space for all those searching and wondering what to do next. For those of us who are thinking, "I'm out of God's grace," this is a place we can say to each other, "You aren't. He's with you every step."

Because life is more dynamic than those systems allow.

God is more expansive than the rigid boundaries we've insisted he be confined to.

I hope that sharing this story will allow people to see the signs earlier than I did, to make the changes before it all collapses so completely at their feet. Or that someone who has already had that happen will read this, and they will hear me say, "I understand. I understand that you are doing everything you know to try to make something good come out of this, and it keeps deteriorating. It keeps going the other way. But it won't always be that way."

I hope that people will understand that, even after straying, even after a fall, even after losing faith, we can live richly and without fear. We can broaden ourselves, liberate ourselves, release ourselves from that quiet harbor and visit the expansive world.

PART I

LOSING MYSELF

CHAPTER 1

WHEN THE WALLS FALL

The signs had been there for years.

For at least a decade, there had been cracks in the veneer I chose to ignore, to gloss over, because allowing myself to acknowledge them would be doubting God, and in Christianity, we leave very little space for doubt. Nevertheless, there were shadows that loomed in the back of my mind—for how long? decades maybe?—because the questions were too big and complicated and impossible to address on my own. I thought that if I just hoped and prayed hard enough, they would go away. God would take care of them.

Of course he would. That's what I had always been taught.

But in August of 2006, I was lost, both personally and professionally, and after a three-day leadership conference at Canyon View Vineyard Church in Grand Junction, Colorado, a church I had founded almost twenty years earlier, I felt broken, hopeless, and alone. I don't remember talking with anyone afterward or leaving or getting in my car, but somehow I found myself at home, where I climbed the stairs to my second-floor bedroom, called a friend, and wept uncontrollably. In an instant, the beliefs I had spent my whole life building and all the certainties about my faith, my career, my marriage, and my life came crashing down.

When I say that I wept, I do not mean a trickle of tears. This was no simple expression of sadness or grief. To be honest, it was almost an out-of-body experience, and there was nothing I could do to stop the overflow of emotions erupting from deep inside. I felt like I was coming apart, and everything inside of me was unraveling, and I remember watching it as if I were outside myself, thinking, *How strange.* I had always considered myself a man's man. My role models were rugged, unemotional men like my father and my uncle, who was the local high school football and wrestling coach. Like them, I kept my emotions at bay and tried to be strong, unflappable, and brave in the face of conflict or hardship. Even my interests were "manly": I loved motorcycles and sports cars and eating steaks and cheeseburgers.

Yet there I was, weeping, brokenhearted, and vulnerable. It's difficult to express in words how despondent I was, how unhinged I felt. I wondered if I wasn't having an absolute physical, mental, and emotional breakdown.

Both personal and professional circumstances had contributed to the breakdown. For several years, I had been struggling under the weight of a megachurch, watching Canyon View Vineyard grow but knowing that I was overwhelmed by the increasing responsibility and the amount of management and administration it required. At home things weren't any better. I had been praying and fasting for ten years for my wife, who was stricken with multiple sclerosis, to be healed of her affliction. I had also sent up countless prayers for the chasm that had grown between us over the course of decades to somehow shrink so we could bridge it and repair our marriage.

But those things hadn't happened, and instead of really taking a hard look at why, I had kept myself busy. I just kept myself moving, constantly in a hurry to do the next thing so that I didn't have to stop and delve into a complex reality, one in which I was struggling and my prayers didn't seem to be working. Part of it was that I wasn't equipped to face that contradiction. So I kept busy, getting to the next meeting, preparing for the next weekend ahead. But as we all know, there is a vast difference between busyness and fulfillment. One may get a certain amount of satisfaction from a full schedule and the sense of importance that accompanies it. Yet at a certain point, keeping up the routine and maintaining the façade began zapping most of my energies. Somehow the same things that used to bring such fulfillment were actually dragging me down to a mere shell of myself. Externally, I tried to look content and be a good person and leader; however, hiding my turmoil became increasingly difficult.

So when I listened to a preacher at the leadership summit talk about reaching a point where he was emotionally, mentally, and physically drained, it was like every word in that message was directed right to my heart and spoken directly to me. It was like he and I were the only ones in the room, and he had all the words I didn't have to describe what I was going through. *You no longer find joy in things that used to bring you happiness. You used to enjoy doing things with your family, but now you don't. You used to enjoy going to work, but now you don't. You can't make decisions, and the simplest tasks become mountains to climb. You have no creative energy, no relational energy, no energy to feel anything at all. You can't sleep at night. You feel numb.*

Given the fact that I had ignored the tensions in my life, it was almost inevitable that it would all come crashing down. But that doesn't change the fact that I was facing the biggest disappointment in my life, and the inconsistencies—between who I thought God was and who I was experiencing God to be, between the life I'd imagined for myself and how I was actually living—were so intense that pain seemed to be my only companion. Everything seemed surreal and misplaced and, at the end of the day, so wrong. I was confused and exhausted, and I simply couldn't continue. So the life I had spent so long building for myself fell, and I felt as though my whole life lay in an ash heap at my feet.

I was numb inside, and I was fighting sleeplessness almost every night, taking Ambien to the point that it was affecting my memory. I was avoiding my friends, my wife, and my colleagues. I dreaded my work, and each week, the thought of coming up with another sermon to satisfy a hungry flock was almost too much to bear. I used to think people who burned out were weak, but suddenly I was there, and I felt empty, isolated, and desperate. I was numb to the core of my being, a person aware of my surroundings but unable to arouse enough energy to care about much of anything. That such awful problems continued to exist in my life after much prayer, devotion, and sacrifice became a real irritation, and I finally had to face what wasn't working with my faith.

But how could this have happened? How could this God I served allow such a downward spiral in my life, such confusion and despair, in *me*, his devout follower?

I had been in church since infancy, I had been a missionary, and I had spent twenty-five years as a pastor. I prayed and tithed and studied Scripture. I believed in the victorious life in Jesus. So to me, this loneliness and this desperation just didn't make sense. They threw up a host of questions that I couldn't evade and I couldn't answer. Where was God in the midst of my storm? What did it mean to believe in a personal relationship with the Divine when he seemed distant and aloof? Where was the strength he gave to overcome all things? Was I the "ye of little faith," despite my belief that I had great faith? I had heard many people going on about God answering their prayers. What was right about their requests—and even more importantly, what was wrong with mine?

I wondered if this experience was unique to me. I knew that life was full of suffering, but I had always been taught that my faith would protect against that. In all of my years being raised in the church and around spiritual teachers, never can I recall a message that talked about the darkness of the soul that men and women of faith have faced. Instead, there was a consistent message of victory:

that faith would always conquer the mountain in front of you.

But once the pain in my own life was real and inescapable, and once my once-certain faith had fallen around me, my paradigm shifted—and it shifted quickly. When I read the Bible in the following weeks and months, I no longer saw only the victorious life in Jesus. I saw that most of the psalms were laments. They are the heartache of the soul, wondering where God is, asking questions about his character. In Psalm 43, the psalmist cries out to God,

> You are God my stronghold.
> Why have you rejected me?
> Why must I go about mourning,
> oppressed by the enemy?

There are dozens more psalms just like this, and in his grief, the psalmist is not alone.

In 2 Corinthians, Paul writes about how much he and his companions suffered in Ephesus. "We were under great pressure far beyond what we were able to endure, so that we despaired of life itself," the great evangelist says. Things were worse than they could endure! To despair of life itself! I never heard much about Paul's despair, and I never delivered a sermon on it either. But throughout ancient writings and in more modern examples, great patriarchs and matriarchs of the Faith attest to the same experience.

Centuries earlier, Job cursed the day he was born.

For obeying God's call to preach, the prophet Jeremiah was imprisoned by the king, and in chapter 20, he too regrets his birth and believes the Lord has deceived him. "Why did I ever come out of my mother's womb?" the prophet cries. "Trouble and sorrow, to end my days in shame."

In the twentieth century, Mother Teresa of Calcutta, in the midst of all her work, penned a prayer of suffering: "Lord, my God, who am I that You should forsake me?... I call, I cling, I want—and there is no One to answer—no One on Whom I can cling—no, No One."[1] Here was a woman so dedicated to her faith that she gave everything away to follow Jesus and serve the sick and the poor, and yet her personal letters reveal that for decades, she felt desperately alone.

Then there was the Lord's own messenger, described in the Gospel of Luke as Jesus' cousin: John the Baptist. His birth, like Isaac's of the Old Testament and Jesus' in the New, was a miraculous birth. He would be the one to prepare the way of the Lord, and in his message for all to repent and be baptized, for the kingdom of heaven was at hand, he filled that role. He amassed hoards of followers—"All of Judea, and the whole region around the Jordan were going out to him," Matthew tells us in his third chapter. Then in Matthew 4, it was John who proclaimed Jesus as the Son of God. After John baptized Jesus in the Jordan, "The heavens were opened, and he saw the Spirit of God descending like a dove and coming upon him. And a voice came from the heavens, saying, 'This is my beloved son, with whom I am well pleased.'"

One would only imagine that, as someone God used to announce his Son, as a man whose message and even how he dressed were reminiscent of the prophet Elijah, as someone working tirelessly to bring about the kingdom of heaven, John would have an inside track to God. John's effectiveness in drawing people to repentance and reverence toward God, it always seemed to me, showed that God was backing his mission and work (and by extension, my effectiveness made me feel that God was backing mine). But then John denounced Herod, the ruler of Judea, for having an affair with his brother's wife. As a consequence, and maybe out of fear of John's power to influence the masses, Herod threw John in jail. To make matters worse, the daughter of Herod's mistress exacted a promise from Herod: that he would give her whatever she wanted. She asked for John's head.

At the time, Jesus was traveling throughout Galilee performing miracles. He healed the centurion's servant and calmed the stormy seas. He allowed the paralytic to walk again and made the deaf hear and the blind see. From prison, John heard of these works and sent a message to Jesus: "Are you the one who is to come, or should we look for another?"[2]

It's a strange question for the man who baptized Jesus, and it wasn't until I felt alone and like God was not answering my most heartfelt prayers that I began to understand this moment with John the Baptist in a new way. I began to imagine John sitting in his cell, knowing he is about to be executed. And the Messiah is traveling around working miracles for strangers and sinners, seemingly ignoring John's plight. Instead of sending a message promising support or rescue or the working of a miracle on John's behalf—something like, "I will save you, you can count on me"—Jesus sends a message confirming all the things he is doing for others, and something that would become a major doctrine of the Christian faith, but does nothing to keep John from dying at the hands of Herod: "The blind regain their sight, the lame walk, the lepers are cleansed, the deaf hear, the dead are raised, and the poor have the good news proclaimed to them." And verse 6 hits the point home. "And blessed is the man who does not fall away on account of me."

I'm not going to do what you are hoping I will do, but don't lose faith.

I imagine the way those words must have rung in John's ears—hollow and disappointing. I imagine John's expectations of who Jesus was and his own special place in the heart of the Lord evaporating instantaneously. I imagine the sinking feeling—*I know the Messiah, and I have done the Lord's work, but he will not rescue me.*

As with the Psalms, as with the disappointments of Paul, as with Jeremiah and Job and Mother Teresa's despair, I suddenly felt that I was in John's shoes, and hearing that these great believers had felt alone and rejected gave me a small bit of peace. My whole life, I'd thought I had an inside track to Jesus, and that my prayers and life were special to God. I believed that if I did the right thing here on earth and obeyed, when it came my hour of need, all my faith and all the work I had done in the name of God would translate into some sort of heavenly brownie points, and God would be there for me. This is what I taught and believed, and maybe we don't usually say it this bluntly, but it isn't uncommon in Christian circles. We earn favor with God. We do what we are supposed to do, and therefore, when we most need him, God will do his part too.

But at his moment of greatest need, John arguably felt the most rejected, alone, and abandoned. I felt the same way. I realized that like John the Baptist, I had no inside track with God. I got no special treatment from heaven just because I was leading a megachurch that was ministering to thousands of people in the name of Jesus.

Why hadn't I paid attention to this darker side of the Scriptures before? Why hadn't I noticed that these great people of faith had experienced such huge caverns and caves, such darkness of the soul? Maybe I, along with countless other pastors, had avoided seeing it because it's depressing and difficult to think that King David felt forsaken by God and oppressed by the enemy. Maybe it's because that darker side doesn't inspire hope or a warm, fuzzy feeling.

Maybe it's because I believed what I wanted to believe, instead of believing what was there.

Over the years, I've come to understand what happened to me that afternoon in August of 2006 and how it fundamentally changed me: I was disillusioned. In that moment of desperation, I saw every certainty I had about God crumble. In the years that have followed, I have been forced to rebuild, and nothing looks the same. I have learned that, contrary to what I was taught and to mainstream Christian opinion, faith is not a neat little package where all of the issues of life are filed in alphabetical order so I can pull them out during any crisis I'm facing. There isn't a prayer to say or a Bible passage to read that will make every problem resolve itself and disappear from view. Life isn't black and white, and I have a much bigger role in determining what my future will be than I ever gave myself before.

The word *disillusionment* has various meanings and conjures many different images. One definition is "the act of disenchanting." To disenchant: to free someone from a spell, to disappoint. That afternoon in August of 2006, both freedom from illusion and disappointment happened at the same time.

When I imagine disillusionment, I think of a bubble bursting. My expectation that all things would "work together for good" had been formed early. Over the years, I clung to that belief, but suddenly, I was surprised to find that in the face of my experience, this belief that was as fragile as a soap bubble, and that something I had sought for so long and had believed so fervently could disappear in a moment.

Still another meaning of the word *disillusionment* is to open someone's eyes. The blinders had fallen away, and immediately I knew that there were beliefs I professed about God that simply did not make sense to me, and maybe they never had. It was painful to see, especially because my religious convictions were so deeply held and were such a part of my identity. But suddenly, I was freed from those belief systems, and I realized that my disillusionment was making changes both externally and internally simultaneously.

There was another element to my disillusionment that was difficult to realize as a fifty-seven-year-old man: I had suddenly lost my innocence. I realized that I had spent my life being naïve, wanting to believe in something that sounded too good to be true. I lost my innocence concerning God, religion, church, marriage, and prayer, and the reality sank in that nothing would ever be simple again.

That may sound depressing, I know. And for a few years after I was cut free from the familiar moorings, things were really difficult.

But ultimately, this is a hopeful message. I can honestly say that I have learned things about myself, the world, and the Lord since my disillusionment that never would have been possible under my old worldview. In exchange for the losses, I have made many gains. I have been able to build my own faith, not one that was formed by others but one I was able to discover in my own heart and mind, something I have been able to reconcile with my own reality. Now, I am able to be honest about God—with myself and others, even with God himself—about his role and whether or not he will intervene in our lives on a daily, weekly, monthly, or yearly basis; about whether he will suspend natural laws for all who ask; about whether the times I thought I heard him speaking to me were really him, when I believed he was connected to me in intimate ways, knowing the hairs of my head and guarding over my life. I believe my disillusionment was a positive unraveling that allowed me to grow away from something that was passive and static toward something active and dynamic.

But it's not over yet. Because I've also come to believe that disillusionment is something that will happen to me again and again as I continue on this journey of discovering who God is.

CHAPTER 2

FOUNDATIONS OF FAITH

Over the past few years, I've asked myself many times, *How does an illusion occur?*

Why do people see what they want to see, but not the reality of what is actually happening in their lives?

To make it more personal, why didn't I want to understand that the pain I experienced in those years leading up to my disillusionment was an indication that something was wrong? Was my faith forcing me to deny what was real, even to the point of ignoring my feelings of disappointment and grief? Did it ask me to put on a pretense that everything was okay?

I pushed these questions down for a long time, but once the walls fell and I finally allowed myself to acknowledge them, it was like the dam had burst, and I was deluged.

With questions like: What do we do when things don't work out the way we thought they would, when we believed God would rescue or deliver us from circumstances and he doesn't?

Like: Is it okay for me to have a crisis of faith where I can discover what I truly believe for myself, not what another person or institution has taught me?

Like: Does the tension we struggle with, about God and suffering and heaven and humanity, become a companion for life? Or can we find a place of faith that is practical, a place of faith that brings comfort and peace?

Becoming a skeptic was something I never imagined, but as time passed, I came to realize that my life circumstances had revealed to me a more realistic picture of the world. Suddenly I realized that I had lived my whole life feeling spiritually superior to everyone else, and that the arrogance of my heart was not only unbelievable, but downright disgusting. And suddenly, I could see *myself*.

If I really go to the heart of it, I wasn't disillusioned with God. I was disillusioned with the institutions we had built as humans, and more than anything, I was disillusioned with *myself*. I realized that I had bought into those human institutions with total and blind faith, and once the blinders had been removed, I felt like I had fallen for the biggest con there was. When that happened, it was a battle for me. I knew that God existed, and yet, in my heart, I knew that the stuff I had been fed my whole life, and the stuff I was feeding others, just didn't work. I felt like a sucker, and I had no idea where to turn, what to believe, or how on earth I could make sense of any of it.

For this to resonate, you probably need to understand the foundations of my beliefs, how deeply they ran, and how much they defined and controlled me. I was born in Grand Junction, Colorado, in 1950, at a time when the dominant philosophy of life was more in tune with a Norman Rockwell painting than what the world really had to offer. I was raised in a home with a homemaker mother and a breadwinning father, and I cannot overstate how loving they were. But my parents came up in the Depression era, so they were very hardworking, hard-nosed individuals, very waste-not-want-not, very strict, and very religious. My mother had a true convert's zeal after "coming to the Lord" in her early adulthood, and my father revered pastors more than any other group of people. Between the two of them, religion was an inescapable reality for my sister and me.

We attended a rigidly fundamentalist church in Grand Junction. We were there *all the time,* and there was never a question of whether we'd go. It was a given that we'd be there every time the doors were open. We went to church on Sunday morning and Sunday night. We went to Tuesday night prayer and Thursday night Bible study. We were even there on Saturday nights for choir practice. This institution became the light and the beacon and the womb and the source of all nourishment for me. It was the lens through which I saw the world. And because it was the only thing I knew, and because it was so familiar, it was comfortable. It was home.

My relationship to this church was and still is complex. It was at church that I had my first real "encounter" with God, an encounter that remains the anchor of my faith in God. Of that night itself, I remember very little, only that it was a Tuesday night prayer meeting and I was probably eight or nine years old. Usually on Tuesday nights, there would be a little singing at the beginning, and our fiery, charismatic preacher would roam the main aisle a little, giving a few words of direction. Then everyone would start to pray.

That night, I don't remember the songs or what the pastor said or anything the others were praying about, but suddenly, I was filled with a feeling of peace. I felt washed and cleansed, and if you'll forgive the cliché, like I was walking on air. I somehow knew that I was encountering Christ, and I had the distinct sense that my experience was a real, measurable phenomenon. Cognitively, there is nothing that I can point to and say, "This is what it was," but I encountered something that night that radically changed my life. After that, despite the fact that I was an eight- or nine-year-old boy whose main interest was playing football or tag at recess, I actually began taking my Bible to school and would read it instead. Something fundamentally changed in me that Tuesday night.

But the rest of my experience in church was not as euphoric. The church was a fundamentalist enclave that emphasized who was "in" or "out." Salvation was important, as was baptism, and we believed in the Trinity, though one person was emphasized over the others: more than anything, our pastors spoke about the God of the Old Testament, the Judge, the Ruler, the authoritarian, the distant one. He was the one who could throw you into hell, so of course, you wanted to please him. Truthfully, I was scared of God.

Jesus, I liked. I always felt drawn to Jesus, and it was hard for me to put together how Jesus and God could have been one. Father and Son? It just didn't add up. I could identify with Jesus; he seemed so loving and warm. What he did in the New Testament—feeding people, healing people, speaking kind words to them—made me want to be around him. He was the image of compassion: telling others not to judge, and drawing the line in the sand with the crowd who wanted to stone the adulterous woman, then saying, "Go and sin no more." But though his grace was mentioned sometimes, I wasn't taught a whole lot about it. It was always the austere God that came through, not gracious Jesus.

As for the Holy Spirit, that person was mysterious, and something to be experienced. It wasn't the dove or the flame, though we knew of those symbols. The Holy Spirit was more about power, demonstrated through speaking in tongues and the interpretation of tongues. Through those gifts, there would be an immense power in your life. But really, speaking in tongues was an end in itself. The experience itself was so heavily emphasized that how the rest of that power manifested in your life wasn't really important. It didn't matter whether you gained a lot of money or lost your job the next week. Speaking in tongues just showed that you were chosen—that you were in.

Members of our church lived a separate life from the rest of the community, and there were lots of rules about our behavior. We didn't go to dances or to the movies. We didn't drink or go to bars. We certainly didn't curse, and we had a very puritanical relationship with sex. The rules really seemed to pervade every part of our life, and there was a sense that, even at an early age, we were *better than.* It was arrogant, but we truly felt that we were superior to everyone else, whether they were Christians or not, because we kept these rules.

One of the reasons we followed these rules was because our theology said that if we lived these rules, our lives would be good, and if your children follow them, then your children would turn out right. But our church was also very focused on eschatology, or how the world would end. We believed that true Christians would be taken away before the trials and tribulations of the book of Revelation, and in order to make sure you were not left behind, you had to mind the rules at all times. Woe to the one who was caught breaking the rules when the Rapture occurred! Woe to the one who wasn't on guard when the Master returned!

So as a child, it was as if hell was scared out of you.

Even so, there were no guarantees, and sometimes children slip up. You can imagine the tiny rules children break—stealing a pencil, saying a curse word on the playground, or any number of things that kids do in the process of growing up. But those weren't so trivial to the kids at our church, because if that day you got home from school and nobody was in the house, you would just absolutely melt in fear because you thought people had been raptured and you hadn't made it.

I can remember the day it happened to me. Usually, I'd get home from school in the afternoon, and my mom would be there, already cooking dinner, coming to greet me at the door to ask about my day at school. Yet that day, the lights were off and the house was quiet, with no savory smells emanating from the kitchen.

I was shocked; I thought, *I've missed it.* I ran into every bedroom, yelling for my mom and hoping I'd find someone. As I passed through each empty room of our small home and finally determined that I was alone, my stress level grew until I was filled with absolute, stark fear. Immediately, I began wondering about what life would be like without these people around. It was terrifying. The home that was a place of comfort and security was suddenly almost an abyss. I can distinctly remember thinking, *I've gotta live the rest of my life without my parents or my sister or my relatives.*

My sister had the same experience: of stepping through the front door, calling for my parents, and being stricken with the thought that she was all on her own. Many friends of mine who attended my church recall having the exact same experience and feeling wretchedly alone.

Of course, nobody really talked about how that might affect a child's psyche.

In fact, they didn't question what the church, and especially the pastor, was saying at all. Some of that was due to the era. Our church was organized with the pastor as the head honcho, and in the late fifties and very early sixties, people weren't yet challenging authority on a widespread scale. But it was also our mentality in the church. The pastor was the ultimate authority, with knowledge of Scripture and a main line to God, and we believed that whatever he said was true. You didn't question; you became an automaton. Even asking a question outside the bounds of what the church taught almost labeled you as a rebel, as a heretic. Any dissenting view was met with a stiff, inflexible, written-in-stone answer.

And yet all of us had those kinds of questions in our hearts.

Developmental psychologists have terms for this: as children, we were *assigned* the identity of Christians, specifically this fundamentalist, charismatic sect of Christianity, instead of developing our own identities as individuals. And this assigned identity was something I carried for most of my life. I believed what was in front of me because I didn't really have an option not to—I felt like I had to obey my parents, and the alternative to believing what my church taught was eternal damnation. Even if my religion changed—and I did move away from the charismatic church of my childhood into Youth With A Mission, which was more open and inclusive, and finally into the Vineyard Movement—I never truly questioned Christian orthodoxy. I never went through the process of developing my own belief system after finding myself in a spiritual crisis and exploring other options. What most people do in adolescence or early adulthood, I found myself doing at the age of fifty-seven, as a burned-out, broken-down senior pastor whose life had spiraled out of control.

As I've said before, it's not that there were never cracks or that the shadows of uncertainty never hung around. But early on in my life, I stifled the questions that began to arise because remaining loyal to the church and its teachings was more important. That didn't mean those questions went away. During my adolescence, the theory of evolution was coming to the forefront of the culture, and I realized that not everybody believed in the Bible. I was totally dumbfounded, but I had no way to process this new information. The whole conflict between science and faith was complicated and nuanced, but we were secluded from the conversation altogether. Our parents and our pastor would just patch together simple explanations that didn't really satisfy, and I was put in a place where I was not able to explain or articulate what I believed when my friends would ask me questions.

More than anything, my social interactions confused me. It was easy to demonize a group of "godless" scientists in some Ivy League institution, but from junior high on, I had many friends who were good people but didn't attend my church, and they seemed to be having such a good time in life. In my heart, I wished to be like them. I wished I didn't have to go to church all the time and that I could go to the movies or to a school dance. But in our strict theology, those people were on a different road than we were, and those people weren't going to make it to heaven. They were not bad people—many were actually churchgoers—but in our framework, because they didn't observe the same rules and regulations that we did, and because they weren't as "holy" as we were, they were out and we were in. Yet, instead of making me feel secure, this always made me uncomfortable.

It was also difficult because my friends would want to come to church with me and see what was going on there, but I was always nervous because I knew how strange it would appear to someone outside our faith. Once a friend asked me if he could visit, and I thought, *Okay, I'll take him to Thursday night Bible study, and we'll sit up in the balcony.* I was sure that no one would break out in tongues at Bible study, and surely not up in the balcony. So he came, and we climbed up to the balcony and sat down, and the preacher began. Soon enough, a lady near us in the balcony began speaking in tongues. I almost fell out of my seat. When he turned to me and asked what was happening, I could only shrug my shoulders and say, "I don't know."

How to explain what was going on? I had no words for that. It was just how it was done. It was just what happened.

In high school, I finally got the courage to invite my girlfriend, Cheryl, who would become my wife, to my church. The first time I took her, a famous Pentecostal preacher was visiting. He delivered an intense hellfire-and-brimstone message—a real "turn or burn"—then called out a couple of guys, who began speaking in tongues. At the end, he invited people down for a massive altar call. Cheryl and I began walking down, and she was so scared she walked right out the side door. Later we went out to dinner with my parents and my aunt and my uncle, and while they chatted about how wonderful the service was, she sat silently. She was so upset she couldn't eat.

This was the paradox: that even though we were "in," I always felt relegated to the position of an outsider at school or in the larger community. I also felt like I had to defend my peculiar religion, though without the necessary skills. Once, when I was about ten years old, I was invited to a birthday party, and part of the celebration was going to the movies. I lied and said I had a dentist appointment so I didn't have to explain that my religion prohibited it, but I wanted to go in the worst way. Remember, in those days all we had was black-and-white TV. The signal didn't come on until 3:30 in the afternoon, and it was a test pattern. But television was such a novelty that we would sit around and watch the test pattern. So to think about being in a theater with that huge screen!

I felt entirely left out, and I didn't understand why we were sequestered in that way. I can remember trying to explain to my peers why we couldn't go to shows and feeling like a dummy on the knee of a ventriloquist. I'd say something that my pastor had told us about how Hollywood was full of bad people and we didn't condone what they stood for, but I was spewing out answers that were as perplexing to me as to my friends, especially since we really didn't know what people in Hollywood were doing or what they stood for. (The irony was that everyone in our church who could afford one had a TV. They watched everything they could, as if TV came from a different place. Somehow nobody saw the contradiction.)

But we know how things go with forbidden fruit, and eventually, my desire to be with my peers won out. My junior year of high school, I decided to go on a double date to the Rocket Drive-In on North Avenue with Cheryl and another couple, and not only did I agree to go along, but I drove my two-door, green-and-white '56 Chevy coupe, which my summer savings of $130 had purchased.

Even remembering that moment over forty years later, I feel like a giddy sixteen-year-old. I was excited about being with my peers and part of contemporary culture. I was elated by the novelty of it all. It was so new to me that I didn't even know what the speaker was, and Cheryl and the others had to grab the silver box and show me how to hang it on the window so that we could hear the show.

It was strange, but it definitely didn't feel wrong. On the contrary, it felt fun and exhilarating. What a strange dichotomy! Instead of evil, it felt wholesome, and I enjoyed the movie and the company I was with. I was only worried I would get caught, that someone would see me, recognize my car, and tell my parents.

The fear of getting caught that evening was a microcosm for how we lived: trying to appear good on the outside, to say all the right things and be all the right places. The irony is that you can learn the language and the habits, but that doesn't mean you have a heart for what you're espousing, and living someone else's convictions means your heart may never be transfixed by a dynamic relationship with God.

For me, the separation from the world was a great conflict. I was attracted to what was happening in the world, and I liked what I felt when I was hanging around people who didn't go to my church. I liked the parties, I liked the music, and I liked to watch people dance, though I wasn't a good dancer myself. I remember watching all of my friends at the Lincoln Park Barn, a community center where they held dances in the summertime, and thinking, *They are just having fun. There's nothing bad happening here.* It made me realize the rigidity of the life I was leading, in contrast to the freedom and the fun these kids had.

Another time, I went bowling with my friend Eddie and his mother, Connie. Bowling was off-limits for us for some reason, though I can't remember why. I was eleven years old, and even at that age I realized, *This is good. This is fun.* I watched Eddie and his mom laughing together, and I knew they weren't doing anything wrong. They weren't these dark and wicked people like my church had taught. They weren't ignorant about their faith or the ways of God, and they weren't doing anything that ruffled their consciences.

Truthfully, their actions didn't bother my conscience either. I frankly had more fun with my nonchurch friends than with anyone from my congregation, and it wasn't that we were transgressing. It just seemed like we had more authentic relationships where we were engaged with the culture and issues of the day. These were good people, and I couldn't understand why there was such a division between *us* and *them.*

I remember feeling like there were two people residing in me simultaneously, and I thought one of these creatures was evil and the other one was good. In my heart, I knew that going to the movies wasn't evil. I knew that dancing and listening to popular music weren't wrong. In fact, I loved the music of my youth. Growing up in the sixties was an exciting time for many reasons, but the music was hard to beat. Bands like the Beatles, Led Zeppelin, the Mamas and the Papas, and Three Dog Night were popping up left and right. It's hard to overstate how much I loved listening to these new and exciting bands. (Even now, decades later, my iPod is filled with their albums.) Of course, there are certain behaviors one should avoid, with good reason. But listening to the Mamas and the Papas was not breaking one of the Ten Commandments. As a teenager, it felt like I was living in a straitjacket. It was also confusing because no pang of conscience accompanied an afternoon of listening to secular music. Instead, I would listen to this kind of music every time I had a chance and simply hope I didn't get caught. Was this side of me dark? Was this side of me that wanted to dance, or run around with my friends, wrong? Were the people who did those things damned to hell? I didn't think so, but my authority figures said it was so, and I felt I had no other choice than to accept what they said.

Given my home life, this isn't exactly surprising. In 1960, two sociologists conducted a study about rebellion and conformity in young people with regard to religion. The results showed that when both parents agreed on the same religious ideology, the majority of young people conformed to that religious ideology. It's as if the parents' agreement produces a certainty that is difficult for the child to break through, and even if their ideology is different from that of the mainstream culture, the young person is more likely to conform to their parents' belief than what's happening in the greater culture.

I found myself caught in that tension: I wanted to be a part of the world, but more than that, I felt I had to obey my parents and the teachings of the church. To merge these differences was nearly impossible, so what did I do? I conformed to the church rather than allowing my conscience to lead me.

While I don't want to discount my own responsibility for my choices, I think the fact that we weren't encouraged to be inquisitive or to think in a complex way about our faith affected me. I wasn't able to articulate this conflict, and I didn't have the tools to work through it on my own. It was as if the tough decisions I needed to make were being made for me, and in a way that left me stunted. It's what developmental psychologists call a *foreclosed identity,* when a young person is committed to an ideology without the benefit of exploration. Psychologists don't consider this a "true" identity, and it isn't as likely to become intrinsically worthwhile to the young person.

I wasn't the only one in this boat. My church peers and I were schizophrenic, playing a game that separated us from ourselves. Many of the teenagers would attend Saturday night choir practice, then head out on dates afterward, often to the movie theater. It was easy to get in without being discovered, since the theater was dark, but when the lights came on at the end, about half the choir was there. (And you better believe we were all praying that Jesus didn't return at that moment!) What that says to me is that our religion *wasn't* intrinsically meaningful to us—we conformed only externally.

And at our church, like in many, many other Christian communities even to this day, the external meant far more than what was working in somebody's heart. Were you at the right places at the right time? Were you at church on Sunday? If not, the telephone calls would begin: What's happening? Are you okay? Why weren't you there, wearing the right three-piece suit, the right bouffant hairdo?

As I got older and that early Tuesday night experience with God didn't return, I began to feel that it was all just a show, and though I probably wouldn't have said it this way, I felt trapped. I didn't know that I could be part of my peer group and still live a faithful life. I didn't realize that I could have a faith beyond strict, fundamentalist adherence to a narrow interpretation of the Bible. I was trapped in a mindset that basically rendered every other paradigm about God or the Scriptures as invalid, and because God was confined to such strict parameters, I couldn't entertain anything more fluid and expansive, and I couldn't acknowledge my doubts. Even though Jesus cried, "My God, my God," and even though David did the same in the Psalms, for me to question God was not permissible.

Everything was black and white.

Everything had an answer.

Even when the answer didn't satisfy.

If you had seen me toward the end of high school and my first year of college, you probably wouldn't have guessed that I would become a pastor. As I grew older, my heart drifted further away from church, and by extension, from God. In college I was attending church rarely, and with all my professors and their scientific evidence explaining evolution, I was just confused. It was easier to step back and make no moves than to really work this stuff out.

In high school I played football, wrestled, and ran track. My academics were pretty poor, not because I didn't have a brain, but because I had a one-track mind for sports, particularly football. I was contacted by Colorado University my junior and senior years and was on the path to a scholarship there, but my grades were not good enough to get in. So I went to Mesa College in Grand Junction, which at the time was a sort of farm program for Colorado, with the goal of transferring after I had gotten my grades up. I was still dating Cheryl, and she was attending Colorado State University. We got engaged in the summer of 1970 and planned on getting married when we finished college, a few years down the road.

But that fall, a couple of things happened that shifted our trajectory. First, I injured my ankle badly enough to be out for the season. Second, some friends who had joined Youth With A Mission returned to Western Colorado to share the amazing things they had been doing. Our friend Lynn Green spoke about studying in Switzerland and doing mission work in Kabul, Afghanistan, and about how his life had been transformed. When he invited us to be a part of YWAM and see the world, I remember thinking, "Why not?" I was skeptical that someone like me could really be a part of the group, but I didn't have any plans for my life, and since football was over for me, I thought it might be fun.

As for Cheryl, she was even more enthusiastic about YWAM than I was. She had grown up in church in a nominal way, but one night toward the end of high school, she came to my home church with me and had a real conversion experience. She asked to be filled with the Spirit, and she was, and her life was dramatically changed by it. When she went to college, she got involved with Campus Crusade for Christ. She went to a little church there, and though she was nearly penniless, she still tithed.

So when we were presented this opportunity, Cheryl and I decided to get married and go. We got married in December of 1970, and ten days later we were in Lausanne, Switzerland, in the second School of Evangelism (an early version of their Discipleship Training School) that YWAM had ever offered.

When I joined YWAM, I joined so that I could see the world. I didn't do it to be a missionary. At the time, I was not living for God, but I could say the right things at the right time, and I was trained to even *think* the right things at the right time, and I could pull the wool over almost anybody's eyes.

But when I got to Lausanne and I started hearing some of the teachings, my mind was like a sponge. I heard people giving explanations that were nuanced and complex: about the limited foreknowledge of God—about parts of the Scriptures where God didn't know something; about physical depravity versus moral depravity—that we are born into sin but we are not born with sin in us; about human brokenness—how David committed adultery and Paul may have committed murder, but God seemed to redeem all those mistakes that we make. Even though some of the teachings might not make sense to me now like they did then, these were exciting discussions, exciting possibilities, and it was so nice to realize that God was not some harsh, judgmental authoritarian. Instead, he was loving and accessible. I thought, *I can give my life to a God like this.* It was as if I had been wired to engage this way, and suddenly all these little lightbulbs started going off in my head.

I also found it appealing that the Bible wasn't being used for emotionally manipulative purposes. Instead, our leaders encouraged us to be far more contemplative, to read and see what struck our hearts, to go to our rooms and think about what we had heard. It was so much more meaningful than having everybody head down to the front to say "Yeah," and "What a great sermon" and "I agree with ya." It felt like there was meat to their theology and inspired contemplation of the Scriptures, which was a major contrast to "Just believe."

There were also camaraderie and community. Loren Cunningham had founded YWAM after having a vision of young people emerging from the shores of the oceans carrying Bibles, spreading the Good News over all the land. We felt part of a movement, a noble movement. The experience in Lausanne reinvigorated me toward the whole Christian scene and brought a renewing, or a recommitment, if you want to call it that.

In the spring of 1971, we finished our training, which was primarily focused on apologetics, and began a trip across the Middle East, following the teachings and writings of Paul through Greece and Turkey and to the Holy Land. Then we headed out for Afghanistan from June through September. The "hippie trail" of those days started in Northern Africa and worked itself through Turkey and the Middle East, through Iran, and into Afghanistan. Those following the trail were mostly young Westerners, many of them American, and they were looking for truth and meaning. Here's the paradox: no generation before them in the history of America, and maybe the world, ever had as much blessing, materially and financially, as this generation did. Yet they were rebelling. They were leaving everything behind and hitchhiking across Afghanistan, where it would sometimes reach 110 or 115 degrees. There were dangers—being eaten alive by amoebic dysentery, for one—but these were true hippies, really searching out the existential questions about life and God through a completely different lens than they had been offered in America. In Afghanistan, they could basically live a life with no restraints while they explored Eastern culture and religion, and they could experiment with drugs and everything else as a means to that end. We spent three months hoping to win the hearts of these seekers for Jesus, with varied success.

After we got back from Afghanistan, we went to Germany with YWAM and started opening up coffeehouses. People wanted to sit around and talk about Vietnam and race relations and gender equality and all the issues that were becoming so prominent, so YWAM would open a coffeehouse and provide free coffee, hoping to bring Jesus into these discussions. A large portion of the people we saw were American soldiers stationed in Germany. The American military was happy to have us because there was such a huge drug problem with soldiers in their ranks, and they thought we could help these guys deal with whatever they were struggling with. Interestingly, these soldiers were having the same issues we were seeing with the kids in Afghanistan—they were asking the same questions, they were getting hooked on the same drugs. The only difference was that they had short hair and wore army fatigues.

Though Cheryl and I had never done drugs, these were very much our peers, and the more we were exposed to this subculture, the more I kept thinking, *What is missing from our message and our way of life?* I have come to believe that my parents' generation, who came through the Great Depression and two World Wars, were so focused on giving their kids a better life that they went to work and tried to provide a perfect-looking life by materialistic means. The kids were saying, "I don't want your money. I don't want this perfect life. I want you. I want relationship."

Of course, in YWAM we believed that our message about Christ spoke to a lot of the issues these young people were confronting. And in my heart, I developed an understanding about why I had always been so attracted to the counter-culture, why these people were making such an impact on me, why I loved our generation's music and had always wanted to be a part of the world.

I began to believe that part of my faith walk and part of my calling was to help the unchurched come to know God.

At twenty-one, I thought I had cracked open the shell and gotten to the kernel. I was married and had seen the world. I had the answers. Through YWAM, I had found a God I could relate to, a God who loved me, who had known me before I was born, who knit me in my mother's womb and wanted to give me the desires of my heart. And yet I didn't make a clean break from my past. In hindsight, those YWAM years expanded my theological horizons just enough that I could sustain the old ways without having to walk away. Cheryl and I went back to Grand Junction in December of 1971, and we began attending the church of my childhood again, which allowed for harmony with my parents and the community. It allowed me to preserve my worldview, which was flawed but comfortable. I went into the used-car business with my dad, who had been selling old Chevys and Fords since I was a boy.

And the current just kept sweeping me along. When our church suffered a classic church split, about three hundred of us left and began attending the Pentecostal Church of God, which our family stuck with as it split again and again. Pastors came and went, and during one of those periods where there was no one to preach, some people in the church asked me to fill in until they could find someone. So in June of 1981, I began to preach on Sunday mornings to our little flock of only a few dozen. I overprepared and spoke too long, and I am sure I went on tangents and down rabbit trails that tried the patience of every person in the congregation, but somehow they stuck around and let me figure it out.

Two years later, they hadn't found a pastor, the church was growing, and instead of forming a search committee, they gave me what Cheryl called a "field promotion." Until 1986, I continued to sell cars six days a week and preached on Sunday at what we named the Christian Life Center. Twenty years later, our tiny church had grown into Canyon View Vineyard, which by 2006 had sixty-five hundred members on the roles and a yearly budget of $3.5 million. And as the senior pastor, I had all of the trappings that went with it: respect and esteem in the community, a reputation as a man of God, and the pressure of keeping up appearances.

But despite the passage of years, I still couldn't face my doubts. I still couldn't question God. I still toed the line, and I kept a death grip on my inherited theology even when reality seemed to contradict every teaching I had ever learned. The illusion was so ingrained from childhood, so heavily reinforced by family and culture, and so terrifying to abandon that it was easier to simply ignore the contradictions.

CHAPTER 3

WHAT NEEDS TO BE REDEEMED

For the year following my breakdown in August of 2006, I was doing all I could to keep my head above water, to move from one day to the next, hoping that I could keep a lid on the absolute and unrecognizable mess that my life had become.

That season of my life has revealed to me that one of the biggest problems we have in the church is pretense. It's one of the greatest barriers to self-awareness and to knowledge of God, but it's everywhere in the church. That pretense comes in many forms. I know people who have continued to attend the same church for years even though they are bored out of their minds, even when it feels empty and unsatisfying, even though they have heard the same sermons so many times that they know before the pastor begins what he is going to say. But they keep going because they are afraid of what others will say if they don't show up.

Or I know people who have no trouble having a glass of wine at home, but who would never take a sip in public. They'd go so far as to hide any bottles of beer or wine in their home if another member of their church was coming over, and certainly if I, a pastor, were to show up.

Or they wake up every day in a marriage that is completely broken, where they are completely miserable, but they put on a smile and act as if they are not dying inside. They show up at church services and events side by side, as if everything is fine, as if they hadn't been screaming at each other in the car the entire way there.

I shouldn't say "they." I should say "I," because for so much of my life, and especially the last few years of my marriage and ministry, I was guilty of pretending as much as anybody. Between my upbringing and my responsibilities as the pastor of a large, evangelical Christian church, I felt immense pressure to be a strong man who did everything right—to hide my emotions, to live the prescribed life, to do things "God's way." I thought it was important to be a model to my family, friends, and congregation, not only to provide an example, but also so that I was above reproach. I could not be a stumbling block.

And of course, I was still under the illusion that if I did these things, that if I lived God's way, he would give me the abundant life that was promised in the Bible, he would make my path straight and easy, and he would solve all my problems.

I cannot overstate this simple fact. *I truly believed for almost all of my life the lesson from my childhood: that if I followed the right path, everything in my life would end up as perfect as a picture.* I believed it even though my personal experience was contradicting that theology.

But the idea that Christians will have an easy road to hoe if they have enough faith, say the right prayers, and attend the right church is simply untrue. It wasn't true for our matriarchs and patriarchs in the Bible, it's not true in the world around us, and it's not even what the Bible promises us. Good Christian people fall ill with cancer and multiple sclerosis and die in car accidents. Good Christian people lose their jobs and have their homes foreclosed on. Good Christian people face temptation and fall victim to it.

But for whatever reason—maybe to make Christianity an easier sell, or to convince us that the sacrifices we had to make were actually worth it—I was taught that my faith would make my road easier in a very literal way. My paradigm didn't admit the possibility that I would do things "God's way" but still have to endure immense pain and hardship, and it certainly didn't teach me that God might not answer my prayers in the way I wanted him to. It didn't teach me that I might pray and fast for years for a solution to a problem that might never be resolved, and it didn't teach me that sometimes, I had to make decisions on my own.

So when problems surfaced in my life, two things happened.

One, I pretended to the outside world that they weren't there. I felt that revealing my pain and suffering, revealing my own shortcomings and the mistakes I had made in my marriage, revealing that Cheryl and I had reached a place where we simply sucked the life out of one another, revealing that I was burned out in the worst way and needed a long period to rest and recuperate—these things were not possibilities. Because if I told anyone how much suffering I was experiencing, then the image of the victorious life in Jesus would be broken, and I would have to admit that I had been sold a bill of goods.

The second thing that happened was that I avoided taking responsibility for my life, and instead I expected God to work things out. I spent weeks, months, and years praying about these things, thinking that God would fix them. I believed that God was eager to come to my aid, and that if I waited long enough and had strong faith, he would come through with a solution to Cheryl's illness, my difficulties at work, and our broken marriage.

Yet reality was different from that. Time passed, and there seemed to be nothing but silence from the God I thought was ever present, ever loving, and ever ready to give me the desires of my heart. How many times had I thought, *By this time next year, something will be different,* only to have those dates come and go with no change whatsoever. How foolish to think that God would whisk away all my problems when they were with me exactly because *I* needed to figure them out.

Looking back, part of the reason I couldn't act was because I was lost and I was stunted. Within the narrow confines of my inherited worldview, there was no room to make discoveries of my own, or to make decisions based on my own heart rather than what people around me would say. So when I was suffering in a broken marriage that turned our home—what should have been my refuge from the stresses of the world—into a place that was absolute misery, and when my wife Cheryl was terribly ill with multiple sclerosis and her care was an enormous task that I was unable to do on my own, I felt like my only option was to turn to God and plead for his intervention. I had lived this way for almost sixty years, and I wasn't confident in myself to do what my heart and conscience said I needed to do.

Being lost, not knowing who I was, and believing God would solve all my problems led me into the most difficult phase of my life, where I suffered the most pain, where I made the biggest mistakes—but paradoxically, where I finally was able to be open, to be honest, and to live a life of my own design.

Of course, much of this was my own fault.

I was a grown man who should have been able to assert himself and ask for what he needed. It was my fault for not learning who I was or what I believed. It was my fault for being afraid of the judgment of others and trying to dump all my problems on God. It was my fault for avoiding the actions I needed to take for so long that I became desperate enough to act desperately.

I do, however, believe that being raised with such rigid black-and-white thinking, being told what to believe and how to act, shaped a specific mindset in me. And that mindset—which said "These are the rules, there is no in-between, and you must follow the rules or incur the judgment of God and everyone around you"—made it less likely that I would take steps that could have saved me, my family, and people who trusted and believed in me a lot of pain. As a consequence, I hurt many people. I took the steps I needed to take about three years too late, and only after I had committed a serious sin against my family and my God. I only acted when pain was so overwhelming that, like a hand from a hot stove, I finally pulled away.

In 2007, I resigned from my job as pastor at Canyon View Vineyard, and I left my invalid wife. It sounds horrible no matter how I say it.

But it is made so much worse by the fact that I was in love with a woman who was not my wife, and she was in love with me, and she had become my best friend and my confidante. Though we were not physically involved while I was still the pastor at Canyon View, it was still a transgression because emotionally, I was far gone.

I knew what I was doing was wrong and that I was a hypocrite in so many ways. I had spoken so often about the sanctity of marriage and advised many people that they had made a commitment to God and their mate, and that was a sacred covenant. Yet here I was, an adulterer, doing exactly what I had condemned. I was risking my family, my job, and my reputation for this illicit relationship.

The problem was, I didn't care. I had gotten to the point where I was so lonely, in such pain, and so desperate that I would have risked anything to make the hurt go away. I lived in an upstairs bedroom in our house, and my wife lived downstairs. I would lie in bed and think of ways to escape. I even contemplated suicide. Rock bottom may be a cliché, but it's also real, and I had hit it.

I've touched briefly on the difficulties I was having that led to my breakdown on that Sunday night in August of 2006. It had taken a very long time, years of overwhelming stress, a lot of avoidance, and crippling reliance on God's intervention and his perfect timing to get there. At work, I was constantly facing problems that I didn't really know how to fix. I had the responsibility of managing over fifty employees, and I was not a born manager. When people would come to me with problems, I was overwhelmed by the responsibility of having all the answers. Often, I would give them the first solution I could think of, which wasn't always the best, and over time, that led to more problems for me to solve. It was a terrible cycle.

Navigating the different needs and desires of a large congregation was also taking a toll. On every decision I made—from changes in the format of a service, to new policies, to bringing associate pastors on to help relieve the burden of shepherding such a huge flock—I met resistance, either in the form of someone in my office, a flood of e-mails to my inbox, or unsigned letters berating me for something like changing the time of a service. I absolutely hated the conflict.

By the end of my tenure at Canyon View, I would drive to work in the morning, park my car, hurry through the halls of the building, and close my office door as quickly as I could. I did this to avoid the onslaught of employees and members of the congregation who would otherwise step through my door and ask me for something—for money, for solutions, for counsel, for wisdom. All I wanted was to get off the treadmill. I wanted to escape to a place where I wasn't pressed for time, where I wasn't being hounded for ideas, where I had no work and no responsibilities. I wanted to have a job where I didn't have to constantly wrack my brains for answers—digging a ditch, or driving a tractor up and down a field, or driving a truck, where nobody could get to me. At a certain point, the work got so big that I just didn't have the wherewithal for it.

The terrible thing was, my marriage was so intolerable that at an earlier point, church had become my only refuge. Years earlier, as things got worse at home, I had begun using my work as an escape from the difficulties there. Cheryl usually had a home health caregiver at the house with her because she was so ill, and there were always more things to be done at the church. It was an easy excuse—no one argues that a pastor should spend less time doing the Lord's work!—and because we were having so much growth and success, it was exciting.

But suddenly, both places were horrible. The church, that noble endeavor which should have been joyful and rewarding, was absolutely depleting. Our marriage and home, which should have been my sanctuary, were absolutely toxic. Our children had all left home by this point. (Each one moved out almost the day after high school graduation, which is probably an indicator that the tension had been there a long time.) So Cheryl and I were left to our own brokenness. We bickered and fought constantly. On any topic that came up, there was conflict. If I called it black, she'd call it white. If I called it white, she'd call it black. It was exhausting, especially because I felt like I could never win the argument or get her to admit I had a point. She had always been good with words, and she had an incredibly quick wit. She had won "Most Sarcastic" in high school, and when she wanted, that sarcasm could be truly cutting.

Cheryl has passed on due to complications from multiple sclerosis, and I do not want disrespect her life or memory. She was the mother of my children and my partner for thirty-seven years. She helped me build a church that has impacted and inspired thousands of people in their walk with God. But to understand why my life was so unbearable, explaining how she treated me is important. Cheryl was relentlessly critical of me. It wasn't entirely her fault. Her father took his own life when she was pregnant with our second child, Mary, and it understandably devastated her. Eight or nine years later she was diagnosed with multiple sclerosis, which just ravaged her body. We prayed for healing, and she had one period where the disease was inactive, but then it returned with a vengeance. And even though we had literally thousands of people praying for her and "claiming" healing for her, God wasn't granting her healing.

So her father had forsaken her, and her body was betraying her as well, and I think to her—and eventually to me—it seemed like God didn't care. Later a therapist explained to us that the way Cheryl treated me was a way of preparing herself for another trauma. Who would be the next in line to hurt her? Because she believed it would be me, she began actively pushing me away.

To compound matters, the disease had begun affecting her brain, pushing her into more extreme moods and undercutting her desire to make peace or reconcile. Our marriage counselor tried to incorporate this knowledge into our counseling, but it didn't seem to change things. Cheryl was angry about the traumas and hardships in her life and the limitations that she faced because of her disease, and I became the object of her anger. It didn't matter if it was the clothes I wore, if I grew a beard, or the way I cut my hair. It didn't matter if it was the car I wanted to drive, the food I cooked, or the remodel we did on our house to make it easy for Cheryl to get around in her wheelchair. She found fault with everything I did.

It was torture for me, though I know she was miserable as well. One of the most surreal conversations I ever had was when Cheryl and I admitted to one another that we had both wished God would take one of us so that we could be free of the toxic relationship that made us both so wretchedly unhappy. Even through all our counseling and our prayer, we could never find a way to reconcile.

I do not say these things to excuse my infidelity. This is no attempt to rationalize my mistakes, which were of my own choosing, which contradicted my values, and which were solely my fault. I only mean to describe an atmosphere in our home that was exhausting and miserable. As I said earlier, we were in marital counseling, trying to work things out. We had a few close friends who knew how bad things were in our marriage and who tried to support us through this time. Some of our dearest friends brought us on a weeklong retreat, hoping something so intensive could really help us repair our marriage. It seemed promising while we were there, but when we got home, we fell into old routines. Despite the fact that we were "good Christians," despite the fact that we believed in marriage, despite the fact that we had given our lives to the mission of bringing Christ to the unchurched, we could not bridge the gap between us and reach out to one another with love.

I have so much sadness looking back on it. For the first twenty-five years of our marriage, we were a good team, and we had so much blessing around us. We had beautiful, intelligent children whom we adored. We had achieved so much in this relationship, building a family and a mission and seeing so much success with Canyon View Vineyard. But for many reasons—because she was ill and angry, because I withdrew when she lashed out, because we had a mission in our marriage but not true intimacy—we were letting it all go.

In my desperation, I also began to feel a tremendous amount of anger at God for what I was experiencing as a huge and almost palpable absence. Multiple sclerosis was this unwelcome enemy that entered our lives and threw them off course. Why wasn't God coming through with an answer for us? What about his promise in Psalm 103? "Praise the Lord O my soul, and forget not all his benefits, who forgives all your sins, heals all your diseases, delivers your life from the pit, surrounds you with love and compassion." For as long as I could remember, I had pleaded with him for relief from the disease, and as our marriage deteriorated more and more, I pleaded for deliverance from the misery, but nothing was changing. What about that abundant life? When that promise crossed my mind, I could only feel cynical. *If this is life abundant, Lord,* I thought, *you can have it back.*

Honestly, I felt trapped. I felt absolutely trapped in every way. After a lifetime of seeing myself as a provider and protector, I was in a position where I felt inadequate and helpless. If the healing wasn't coming, the counseling wasn't helping, and the prayer wasn't working, what else could I do? The pastor of a huge church divorcing his invalid wife was unthinkable. Really and truly, it was something I could barely even allow to flit across my mind. What would happen to my credibility as a pastor, and what would happen to our reputation in the community? What a hypocrite I would be! To stand up and say I was getting a divorce after talking for so long about how God stands for marriage! To say, "Well, this one just didn't work," after telling so many people they had a responsibility to stick it out! I couldn't imagine admitting that my marriage had failed to a group of people who put a huge amount of psychological and emotional weight into the institution of marriage, a weight that was not only an individual value but part of the cultural and collective values that had grown over centuries. To be the pastor—in many ways the foremost example of what it means to live a Christian life—who undercut an institution that people assigned such deep and heartfelt meaning to was unconscionable. The few times I thought about it, I would feel physically sick.

The only other plan I could see was to ease some of the burden of Cheryl's caretaking, which was my responsibility when I wasn't at work, by finding long-term assisted living for her. Of course, that option was unpopular with all our friends and family, especially with my children. But here was a woman in her midfifties who needed care beyond what I was able to give. I longed for the help, but I hated myself for the fact that I was breaking under this responsibility. I berated myself for being so immature, for being a rotten scoundrel, for my weakness in this ordeal.

With the type of thinking I had then—with a narrow mindset about divorce and how worried I was about the reactions of others—I *was* trapped. I was trapped by that mindset. If I had realized that life was not black and white, I might have admitted that the marriage was toxic for both of us and that we needed to separate. We could have taken steps to ensure Cheryl got the care she needed, but not at the expense of my own mental health. It would have been difficult to break the news to our children, and it would have been difficult to break the news to our friends and our community, but it would have been an honest attempt at doing what was good for both of us.

I couldn't do that, so we just bided our time, though each day became more difficult.

During those months and years, I thought to myself often, *How ugly this is going to be when all of this comes to the surface.*

In my very lowest state, when I felt abandoned by God, when I felt despised by my wife, when I felt overwhelmed by and inadequate for my job, there was a person who showed me love and kindness. At that time, it was water in the desert.

In the beginning, we were simply friends. This woman was interested in a certain ministry in our church, so we had the opportunity to spend time together. She was married as well, so it was beyond me to even imagine something happening between us. But humans crave intimacy. The way we deal with our disappointments and our sufferings is through relationships. It's where we find comfort and relief from the difficulties that this life seems to offer at every turn. Soon, we discovered that neither of us had that. Neither of us had any intimacy with our spouse. We both lived upstairs while the other lived down, and we were absolutely, devastatingly lonely. Somehow, we started to talk on the phone.

For years, I had sat across the desk from people in my congregation asking for advice, and they would make all sorts of confessions. Many were people who had committed adultery, and I would listen skeptically, raising my clerical eyebrow as they said, "I didn't mean to fall in love with this person." I believed that people just needed to know the correct principles and to practice the right disciplines, and they would not fall victim to such transgressions. I believed that I, being a pastor, being what I thought was a fully-formed Christian, would never be guilty of such an act. I didn't always say it outright, but in my mind, my judgment fell heavily on what I saw as their sinfulness and weakness.

But suddenly and without intending to, I had fallen in love with this woman. Just describing it, I use the confessors' words exactly: "I didn't mean to fall in love with her."

I was not above such weakness, and after all my years of devout Christian living, I was not immune to such a fall.

As we all know, love—especially the initial phase of romantic love—has a tendency to make people do things they wouldn't normally do. At that time, love seemed to hijack my brain, and everything else became secondary. Though I thought it was absolutely impossible for me to look for solace outside of my marriage, somehow I was spending hours on the telephone with a woman who wasn't my wife, sharing my disappointments and sufferings as well as a newfound sense of joy.

Of course, it was a burdened joy. We carried guilt because of this—we knew what we were doing was a moral wrong. So we would try to cut things off, but going back to life as it was made that reality even more unbearable. In Genesis, it says that Adam was not made to be alone, but that was how I had been living, suffering the hardships of life without a true companion, without a true mate. I was in a marriage that was dead, one that weighed me down like an albatross around my neck, one that offered no relief or joy or companionship. It was realizing that I could no longer live alone that prompted me to end my marriage.

Only when I couldn't take any more was I able to admit that there were flaws in my thinking, that maybe I had been abiding by a worldview that was full of illusions.

Only then was I able to admit that my experience in life was so at odds with my theology that I couldn't live by that theology anymore.

Only then could I take action.

I resigned my position at Canyon View Vineyard and confessed my affair to Cheryl. I also wrote a letter to my congregation where I confessed my transgression and asked for their mercy and forgiveness. After that, I stayed for a few months in the house with Cheryl, and as a last-ditch effort to save our marriage, we went to one more marriage retreat, this one full of pastors who had committed the same sin as I had and whose marriages were also at a breaking point. But that week only proved that we couldn't be resuscitated. So I packed my clothes and told Cheryl I was leaving. A few months after that, we were divorced.

You can probably imagine the reaction from my children and the reaction of our community. Grand Junction and the surrounding towns in the valley only amount to about 140,000 people, and I've lived here all my life. Not to be immodest, but I was a well-known figure. When word got out that I'd had an affair and had left my sick wife, I experienced a true fall from grace. People I had known for decades, even since childhood, wouldn't speak to me. I was *persona non grata* almost everywhere I went. The worst scenario that I could have imagined came true, but strangely, I was so exhausted and depleted and desperate to get out that I just didn't care.

What a strange fact: that I was fifty-seven and had just discovered that I had no idea of who I was or what I believed.

My life became a mission to find those things out. I abandoned all of my religious trappings. I quit going to church and having my quiet times. After a lifetime of rigid doctrine, black-and-white thinking, and a one-size-fits-all faith, I needed a new path that would lead me from my malady, from my stagnation, and encourage me in my spiritual journey. This was a time to completely retool and realize, maybe for the first time, that God might have the mercy and understanding to give me the space for such a transition. Maybe this was a time to recover what I had lost while I was just doing the same things over and over again without realizing that they weren't helping me grow.

All my life, I had been told, "You can't." But I had been waiting for someone to say, "You can." I was finally telling myself *I could.*

I began taking hikes in the incredible canyons and mountains that surround Grand Junction. I got on my motorcycle and headed down the highway. I drank a few beers and felt good about it. And every once in a while, I would feel God smiling on me, I would feel full and at peace, and I would know that I was going to be okay.

I do not want to glamorize or excuse or rationalize the relationship that led me to this place. Having an affair was a terrible and desperate action, and I regret how much hurt I caused in that desperation. The worst victims were my three children, who I hurt beyond what I ever could have imagined and who are still distant from me because of my actions. I also live with the constant fear of how much damage I have done to people who may have turned away from the church because of my hypocrisy.

The problem is that, in the hundreds of times I have gone over this in the past six years, I don't know how else I could have gotten out of such a dire situation. For so long things had been horrible, but I was just unable to do anything to change it. My only two outlets—leaving my wife or leaving the church—were simply not on the table with the mindset I had then. Even after my 2006 breakdown, I had reached for a temporary solution. I took a three-month sabbatical from the church. I traveled to California to rest and to try to make sense of the breakdown and all the questions I was having about God and my faith and my job and my marriage, but when I returned from it, everything was the same. The same problems greeted me. Another nine months passed, where I was exhausted and confused, where I was struggling because the foundations of everything I had thought and believed and built my world around had been shaken to the core. I carried on even though I felt like dying.

The catalyst for me to make the changes I needed in my life was knowing what it felt like to be alive again. I hate that it was an affair that showed me how to be alive. I wish I had done it in a way that displayed integrity, honesty, and maturity.

But after all I've been through, I would not undo what I did if that meant going back to where I was. I know that ending my marriage was the right thing, and every time I drive by Canyon View Vineyard, even as I am awed at the thought of what we built there and glad that people are being spiritually fed there, I am so relieved that I no longer face the pressure of being the senior pastor. I would not go back and give up what I have learned—about myself and God, about love, about what it means to live my life according to my conscience rather than the fear of someone else's judgment.

I do not tell my story because I am proud of how it happened. I do not tell it to excuse my actions or to gain sympathy for my plight. My hope in telling this story is that people will read it and realize their own need for action. Maybe it's in work, maybe in a relationship, maybe in changing churches to find a place that fosters their journey. One of the most important lessons I learned is that I do have free will, and I am self-determined. I have so much more responsibility in my life than I ever imagined.

In the last five years of this journey, I have come to believe that God redeems what needs to be redeemed. I don't believe that God coordinated my affair in order to teach me something, but I believe that he has used it as an opportunity to make me a better man in so many ways. I have lost my old self—the one that was mired in pretense, who was lost in the form of my faith and rigid, doctrinal thinking, and who was judgmental and always worried about the judgment of others—to discover compassion and empathy for my fellow man. I may not have the answers, but I feel free to be honest and open, to be compassionate and tolerant, to be kind and loving. None of these things would have happened without my disillusionment.

After losing the pretense, I learned a lot about the power of honesty. I think about why the twelve-step program is so powerful—because no one is trying to maintain a façade that they are anything less than broken, suffering, striving-to-be-better humans. At the retreat I attended just before my divorce, I remember one man saying, "I feel the safest around broken people." Everyone there nodded in agreement because they knew they felt exactly the same way. What's sad is that, in general, the current state of the church doesn't foster that type of transparency. Since Jesus left the earth, I'm frankly not sure that it ever has.

Yet it was in seeing myself and everyone around me as broken that I came to believe that our brokenness is our strength. I've come to believe that the idea of a flawed healer, a wounded healer, is important. It's important in explaining that this is how we walk this walk. Nobody has been perfected. We're always going to deal with the brokenness. It was painful for me to realize in my late fifties that I had kept myself in a perpetual state of childhood while I deluded myself into thinking I was fully developed. But I've been able to admit that, and I now know I will probably never completely heal from my brokenness in this lifetime.

What a blessing! What a miracle to be able to see myself clearly and to know that God's mercy was—and is—still upon me! What a relief that I can admit that I have feet of clay! Because of these things, I feel so much better equipped to show the love of Christ, because I know what it means to be broken and to abandon those black-and-white answers and admit that sometimes, we find ourselves in a gray area. Some days will be better than others, and some seasons will be more fruitful. That is the human experience that is life, and our path is one where we have countless opportunities to try to recover from that brokenness, to grow up a little bit more, to discover the next turn that might lead us closer to conscious being before God.

Part II

LOSING MY CERTAINTIES, GAINING MY FAITH

CHAPTER 4

PRAYER: FROM GREED TO GRATITUDE

A few years before I was born, my mother and father had a son who was stillborn. Like many parents who lose a child, they were devastated. They already had a daughter, my older sister Vonnie, but this son would have made the family unit seem complete. Instead, they were faced with profound loss.

I think it was particularly difficult for my father, who desperately wanted a son. But his faith was strong, and he didn't give up. He offered up another prayer to God, asking for the blessing of another pregnancy, another boy, and that this boy would live. But his desire was so intense that instead of just asking for this son, he offered some collateral.

You see, my dad was a regular smoker. It was the 1940s, and smoking was a very common habit for men like him—for all men, I guess—but it was at odds with his fundamentalist faith. For the sake of his soul, not to mention his lungs, he needed to quit. So my father promised God that if this prayer were answered, he'd quit smoking. When I was born in 1950, my father thanked God for his son and honored his part of the deal.

According to our family lore, my very entrance into the world was the result of prayer.

To us, prayer had measurable results.

Prayer was powerful. Prayer worked. And throughout my life, that was a belief that was nearly unshakable.

When I was a teenager and in the midst of my doubts regarding our rigid faith, I had few questions about prayer. One summer, I was working on the second gondola lift on Vail Mountain. Vail was a small resort town, so one night I decided to go into Denver for a change of scenery, thinking I'd hang out in the big city and maybe get a hotel room for the night. But while stopped at a stoplight in town, I realized that I really would love to have a friend to see the sights with me. I thought how great it would be to stay with my cousin Brad, who lived in Denver.

Though the city was home to about three-quarters of a million people, and I had no idea where Brad lived and didn't have a phone number to reach him, I closed my eyes and prayed this silly little prayer, asking God to help me find him, as I waited for the light to turn green. Then I lifted my eyes up, and there was Brad in his car right in front of me. I jumped out and caught his attention, and I had a place to stay and company all weekend long. I can still remember it as an incredibly fun weekend, one that felt providential and blessed. I always believed that God had answered my prayer.

In hindsight, what else would I think but that my prayer had been answered? It was entirely consistent with my worldview. I had a need, and God, the source of all miracles and provision, supplied it. My worldview was built around this divine being who cared for his children, much like the story of the children of Israel in Exodus. As they crossed the desert to the Promised Land, God guided and protected them with a fire by night and a cloud by day; he fed and clothed them throughout their journey. Though they were imperfect and complained that Moses had led them astray by bringing them into the desert, God was their refuge and shelter.

The God I understood was also open to their cries. When the children of Israel gathered their precious metals and fashioned them into a golden calf, God threatened to destroy them for their idolatry. But a prayer from Moses intervened. "O Lord," Moses said, "why should your anger burn against your people, whom you brought out of Egypt with great power and a mighty hand? Turn from your fierce anger; relent and do not bring disaster on your people."

What was the result? The Lord heard him and showed mercy on his people.

Moses prayed, and his prayer transformed God's wrath into mercy.

These were the stories that shaped the understanding of prayer in my family and at my childhood church, in Youth With A Mission, and in the evangelical circles where I soon found myself a leader. We read Matthew—chapter 7, verse 7—again and again: "Ask and it will be given to you. Seek and you will find. Knock and the door will be opened to you." Here was Jesus, our Savior and Lord, telling us to just ask him and he'd provide what we needed. The Psalms told us that God wanted to give us the desires of our heart, if only we would be blameless and upright, if we would commit to him, trust in him, and ask.

The idea of prayer moving mountains was particularly resonant for me, being a native of rugged Western Colorado. In Zechariah 4, the Lord of Hosts says,

"Who are you, O great mountain? Before Zerubbabel you shall become a plain." Jesus echoes the same idea in Matthew 17: "If you have faith the size of a mustard seed, you can say to this mountain, 'Move from here to there,' and it will move. Nothing will be impossible for you." The Gospel of Mark uses similar imagery, only there the mountain throws itself into the sea for anyone who believes completely, for anyone without doubt in his heart. It was an amazing idea—completely astounding that the mountain would throw itself into the sea for anyone who fully believed! What power and might was available to those who implored the Divine for aid!

But even with those promises, my hope and trust in the power of prayer didn't really reach its apex until I had a true mountain in my life. That happened when Cheryl was diagnosed with multiple sclerosis. We were in our early thirties and it was obviously a shock, but for a few months, things seemed okay and she was stable. She was pregnant with our third child, our son Jon, and the disease was not progressing because pregnancy somehow staved it off.

But soon after Jon was born, the disease began a vicious attack. She deteriorated quickly, and within a short period of time, she was unable to walk. It was a very difficult time for our family. I can still remember how our oldest daughter, Wendy, who was about eight at the time, burst into tears the first time she saw her mother in a wheelchair. We were in the sanctuary of our little church, and seeing her strong, capable mother so weakened by the disease shook her to her core.

At the time, I was leading a small but vibrant group of believers. We were a faithful, prayerful community, gathering often to make our needs known to God and with fervent belief that they would be answered. We did this because that was the model set out in the Bible. In Matthew 18, Jesus speaks of power in numbers: "Again, I tell you that if two of you on earth agree about anything you ask for, it will be done for you by my Father in heaven." In case your faith is not as big as a mustard seed, it seemed to say, you can gather with others, and together, your faith will be enough.

In the fifth chapter of the book of James, there's more encouragement to pray, this passage even more relevant to Cheryl's condition. "Is any one of you sick?" James writes in his epistle. "He should call the elders of the church to pray over him and anoint him with oil in the name of the Lord. And the prayer offered in faith will make the sick person well; the Lord will raise him up." A few lines later, we were assured our prayers would work: "The prayer of a righteous man is powerful and effective."

Given this mindset, given this framework for prayer, it was inevitable that we should gather together and pray for Cheryl's healing. We had faith, and we had a need that human beings could not satisfy. (There was and still is no cure for multiple sclerosis, and then, in the early 1980s, the treatments were far behind the treatments available now, which can be very effective in slowing the progression of the disease.)

So we gathered at a prayer meeting, and we prayed for hours. We anointed Cheryl's head with oil, as James had advised us to do, and we continued to pray. At some point in the night, Cheryl went off by herself, and a verse came to her from Zechariah: that she would see the glory of God on the fourth day of the ninth month. I'm not sure how it came to her, or really, what that verse was supposed to mean in the context of the whole Scripture. But heartened, she came back to the group and announced this to everyone.

We were bolstered by the word she had received, and we continued to pray until midnight. At that point, everyone in the room seemed to notice a presence, and Cheryl was affected. As she sat in her chair, her legs straightened out and shook for a minute. We were convinced then that God had heard our prayer, and we were filled with hope that we had claimed healing for her. When we finally went home that night, we were exhausted, but more than that, encouraged.

Cheryl's doctor had advised us that she was going to continue to deteriorate, but about two months after our prayer meeting, her health began to improve. It was a joyful and unexpected reality, and even the doctor was surprised that things had changed so quickly. He called her improvement "dramatic remission" and told us it was uncommon but a possibility for people with multiple sclerosis.

Of course, we believed that it was not something that had just happened in the course of the disease, but that in a supernatural way, God had healed her completely. We proclaimed this in our home, in our church, and in our community. We felt it was proof that our prayers worked, and that anything we needed, we could bring before the Lord and he would answer us. It was a pillar of our faith and a theme I spoke about time and time again for the next twenty-five years.

During those years, I practiced what I preached. I had a very fervent prayer life. In the morning, I had devotions, where I would read Scripture, write in my journal, and pray. In the summertime, I would pray while I sat outside watching the sunrise. In the winter, I prayed by the side of our crackling fireplace. I prayed for Cheryl and my children and my friends. I prayed for our nation. I prayed for the church as it grew, for each staff member by name—though eventually there were too many to do that anymore. I prayed for the congregation and the church's finances, and of course, for any crisis we were facing. I prayed for the sermon on Sunday, that God would guide my message and open people's hearts to him. I would cover everything in prayer, often bringing a list of specific needs so I wouldn't forget to ask God for his provision for all of them. I prayed that all these things would happen if it were God's will.

And because I was working for him, and because I kept his commands and followed the prescribed path, I was confident that God's will would be what I needed it to be.

My morning prayer would continue when I got to the church. Our staff met for daily prayer, focusing on the specific needs of our church and congregation. The congregation, too, had organized and frequent prayer. We had a Saturday night prayer meeting after Cheryl's healing that lasted about ten years, praying for people who were ill and any emergent situations that we thought we should direct God's attention to. We had small groups of people praying throughout the week.

We were a praying church.

We left no stone unturned, no need unspoken.

As years passed and my life became more complicated, both in my marriage and in the church, my own prayer life grew more intense. I continued my regular practices, but I also fasted, and I used each time I felt hungry as an opportunity to pray, to ask again for the thing I needed. There were plenty of times I'd pray just driving down the highway, where I would speak to God out loud, while I was driving to the church or home in the evening, or when I was driving myself to a conference a few hours away. I would name all of the areas of my life where I needed divine intervention.

And I persevered with that unshakable certainty about the effectiveness of prayer. When we spoke about the results of prayer, we held up the success stories. We focused on the outcomes where it seemed that prayers had been answered. It's a cycle many pastors and many Christians find themselves in—believing without a doubt that prayer works, not being able to admit when it doesn't—because truthfully, no one wants to hear about the cancer that wasn't cured or the finances that didn't work out. Those stories undercut our idyll of the victorious life in Jesus, and given the certainties we have constructed for ourselves, that just can't be true. It couldn't be that we would follow in David's footsteps, crying out to God, begging God for an answer to his prayer: "Why are you so far from saving me, so far from my cries of anguish?" In our minds, to do so would be to doubt, and there was no room for doubt in our faith.

Of course, we kept no statistics, but in hindsight, I can admit that there were probably just as many prayers that weren't answered as prayers that were. As just one example, I can look back to 1982, when Grand Junction experienced a huge economic downturn. Beginning in the spring of that year, the shale oil industry, a major source of jobs here in Western Colorado, went bust. When Exxon pulled out of the valley in May of that year, over two thousand jobs were lost immediately; they called it Black Sunday. Several thousand more felt the effects as it reverberated through the support industries.

For a community the size of Grand Junction, that was a huge hit. Every week we were praying for more members of our congregation, that they would be able to find a new job in the area, that they wouldn't have to uproot their families and move to a new city and start their lives all over again. But despite our most valiant efforts, an overwhelming number of people were leaving as days and weeks and months passed.

Eventually, I stopped that line of prayer because it was becoming such a focal point that it was drowning out the rest of the concerns of the congregation. At least, that's what I said then. But in fact, I was discouraged, and I was discouraged because the prayers were not being answered, at least not in any way I could see or understand. In those days, maybe because of my youth and my zeal, I really didn't make the connection. But we were asking with true faith that the prayer would be answered, and we were praying together, all raising our voices to God, and we were God-fearing people who tried our hardest to abide by his commands. Yet our prayers were seemingly ineffective.

But we couldn't say that. What would that mean? That we were the "ye of little faith," people who could not summon faith the size of a mustard seed? That we had impure hearts? That we prayed with the wrong motives? None of those things could be true, in our minds. Instead, we ignored the stories that contradicted our belief in the power of prayer. We told ourselves that we were God's beloved, after all; those who professed complete faith in his sovereignty, his goodness, and his might.

And in my life, prayer seemed foolproof. Though others might have struggled and though their unanswered prayers might have cast tiny shadows in the corners of my mind, I willed myself into belief. I focused on how my wife had been healed, how my church was growing, and how fulfilled I felt by the life that I was leading. I was devoted to prayer, and that God wouldn't answer *my* prayers was unthinkable.

And then it wasn't. Sometime in 1991, Cheryl came to me and said she thought the multiple sclerosis was back. I thought, *It can't be.* Ten years had passed without symptoms, yet here was proof: a dropped foot. Again, the disease set in quickly, and she was soon in a wheelchair again, and the disease continued to attack, this time worse than ever.

I think a lot of questions probably started at this point in my life, though I could barely countenance them, even in my mind.

Had God healed her the first time? was one.

Another was, Does God give healing and then take it away? Or was this just one of those things that multiple sclerosis does—attacking then remitting?

I was never able to articulate these questions or confess them. I was never able to say, "This is absolutely devastating to me." Instead, I kept praying. I worked harder and harder, hoping it would force God to heal her again. I intensified many of my spiritual disciplines. I began memorizing even more Scriptures and listened only to Christian music. I worked even harder to be kind and charitable to everyone—in my thoughts, words, and actions—even people I found it difficult to get along with. I began devoting one day a week to prayer and fasting for a miraculous end to Cheryl's illness and suffering. In some ways, I was like my father, bargaining with God—*I'll do this for you, and you can do this for me.* I was so desperate I probably would have tried anything if I'd thought it would compel him to respond.

I was not alone in this effort. Many of our friends and family and members of our congregation were joining me in this prayer, and in some ways, it was reassuring to know that hundreds, if not thousands, were actually praying for Cheryl's healing. If sheer volume of prayer was a way to move God's hand, we really had the numbers on our side. And these people felt confident in their prayer. Over the years, it seemed like everyone I had ever known and even some people I didn't were coming to me with a "word" that Cheryl would be healed. God had told them all, and so it was inevitable.

But impossibly and so confusingly, she continued to deteriorate, even as my prayers became more fervent and more frequent and even as people were claiming healing on her life. It was shocking to watch this progress over a decade.

Despite our best efforts, by 2002 she was severely ill and in severe pain, so her doctor prescribed some medication that did seem to ease her suffering but had a disastrous consequence. Over the course of that treatment, the medication (now off the market) ate a hole in her upper gastrointestinal tract and opened a large artery. She needed sudden surgery to stop the internal bleeding, but she only had a 50 percent chance of making it through the operation.

As I sat in the hospital that night, anticipating the grief that I would feel if she did not make it through the surgery, I remember thinking, *This does not feel like healing.* It felt like the opposite.

After my disillusionment, I'd look back on that moment in the hospital and think of all those people I had told to pray—pray through, and your finances will work out; pray through, and God will sustain your marriage; pray through, and your loved one will be healed. I would relive those moments in my office, their eyes full of pain and their voices frustrated and despairing, saying, "We did what you told us to do, and it didn't work." I would reflect on the countless desperate situations people find themselves in where they plead for God's protection and favor: a mother praying with all of her might that there will be food for her children, only to watch them go to bed hungry again, or families praying for the safety of their sons in combat, asking God for his protection, whose hearts sink as the uniformed officer shows up on their doorstep with a folded flag.

I had done the same, yet here I was, wondering if my wife was going to make it through the night, worried that even if she did, such an invasive procedure would only give the disease an opening to attack again, and even more explosively. I knew that if Cheryl lived through the surgery or died on the operating table, our lives would never be the same. I felt sick, vulnerable, and full of sorrow. I spent the night begging God to act, to change things, to restore the things that were broken, as he had promised.

He had promised it, hadn't he?

Cheryl made it through the night, but neither of us were unscathed. She was so ill and so bitter, and I was exhausted. I began looking around and trying to compare my lot to other people. Were other people really having their prayers answered? Was their healing from God? Were their steady marriages proof of his intervention?

And if I answered *yes* to those, then the questions became more fraught.

Did God favor somebody more than me?

Does he love us all the same?

Why would he answer someone else's prayer over mine?

Every time I heard someone say, "This prayer was answered," it was exasperating, a shot to my insides. *What are they doing right?* I'd ask myself. *And what's wrong with me?*

That was the only explanation I could muster: that it was my fault. I began seeing all of the reasons why God *wouldn't* answer my prayer. It says in the Psalms, "If I regard iniquity in my heart, the Lord won't hear me." I knew I wasn't perfect. I knew that I didn't always love my neighbor, and that I could be selfish even when I tried not to be. I was a human being prone to sin, like all human beings, so of course, God would not answer my prayers.

In James 4, the apostle writes, "You ask with wrong motives, so your prayers are not answered." So I began to question my motives. Was I really asking for Cheryl's healing for her sake? Or was it for my own, so that things could be normal and so I wouldn't have to bear the burden of a seriously ill wife? Could I possibly be that selfish?

And then I began to condemn myself: *I don't even have faith the size of a mustard seed.* If I couldn't gather enough faith for the major source of anguish and trauma in my life, if I couldn't gather enough faith to allow my wife comfort from her pain, what kind of failure was I?

I kept it together externally, but on the inside, holding on to my certainties became more and more tenuous. Each day the discouragement grew, though it would take another four years for it to wash over me in a flood. During that time, when I thought of God, I thought of silence. I thought of absence where once I had believed that God was "a friend that sticks closer than a brother." That verse now seemed empty to me.

I once heard someone say that the opposite of love is not hate, but indifference. That's how I felt when God did not seem to answer my prayers. He seemed unresponsive to my situation—in essence, he had been unresponsive to my prayers for Cheryl for over a decade. Eventually, I had to face reality: that this silence was the norm in my spiritual pilgrimage, and that there would be no fire by night or cloud by day to lead and protect me through this trial.

I've revisited this story so many times in the last decade. In my mind, I've relived many times the days when Cheryl was sick, my insistent prayers for her healing, and the steady unraveling of the core belief that the prayer of a righteous man is effective. (At least prayer as I understood it, as a way to get God to move in your life and give you the things you need.)

That is simply the truth of what happened. My certainty unraveled, because over the course of Cheryl's illness, thousands of people prayed how many prayers? Good, holy people—compassionate, caring, and loving people—prayed again and again. They prayed tens or hundreds of thousands of prayers.

In my head, I cannot square the facts that all of these people wanted this healing, that we believed in God, were faithful to him, and did our best to follow the biblical prescriptions on how to pray, and yet Cheryl was never healed. That's my reality, and I cannot square that reality with the idea that we have the power to call on God to intervene in our lives. I have parsed through every inch of this quandary, and I have had to step away because it simply doesn't make sense to me. As I have said before, my experience is now stronger than my theology.

But there are some things I do feel certain about. I think my rigid thinking about prayer, my certainty that God would give me the desires of my heart if I only asked, made the pain so much worse when the prayer wasn't answered. At that point, I had two things to grieve—that my wife wasn't being healed and the loss of that comforting shield of faith, that idea that God was active in my life as a protector and provider.

I also feel certain that, after many years of blaming myself for the failure of my prayers, it is unhealthy and unproductive to live with that worldview. Viewing unanswered prayer as a failure on my part only compounded the stress of an already stressful situation, further depleting the small reserves of mental and emotional energy I had. It was an incredibly negative and dark place to be, and for simple reasons of self-preservation, I refuse to believe that it was my fault that God didn't respond. Before my infidelity, I conducted a blameless life, and I really believe that my motives in prayer were pure. From the onset of Cheryl's sickness,

I wanted to see her well. Of course, life would have been easier with a healthy wife, but I do believe my primary motivation was my love for her and a true wish for her comfort. I have watched many people suffering with terminal illnesses in hospice. I feel compassion and sorrow for them and for their families. I want the best for them, and I truly believe that what I wanted was what was best for Cheryl. It just didn't happen that way.

That's a reality I can now admit, but in our fervor for things to be different than they are, in our desperation for a different set of circumstances in our lives, Christians often deny the simple facts of reality. We go through all sorts of the mental gymnastics to maintain our certainties about prayer, even when experience seems to directly contradict it. When we have prayed for healing for a loved one with cancer or any other number of afflictions that this life has to offer, and that loved one dies anyway, we say, "God did give her healing." To me, it's delusional to pretend that we were asking for anything other than healing on this earth. We're not honest enough to accept the facts that are in front of us, to say God did not intervene.

The other way we explain it away is by saying, "Everything happens for a reason." I do believe that we learn from what we endure in life, but I cannot believe in a God who would plan for Cheryl and our family to go through that illness and the subsequent destruction of our life and family so that he could teach us something, or that he would allow her to suffer for all of those years in order to bring something about. If that is the truth, then I cannot love that God. Only a few years ago, around the same time that Cheryl passed away, my daughter Wendy lost her baby boy when he was only nine days old. Afterward, she said to me, "I prayed for God to save this baby, and my prayers were as earnest as any time in my life." I still cannot make sense of why God would cause that to happen, why that would be part of a plan.

In my life now, I am around illness and death all the time, and it has hardened this belief in me. I cannot watch a young man or woman in hospice wasting away with cancer and think, *There's probably a good reason for this. God planned this out at the beginning of time so that this young woman could learn something, or so her friends or family could learn something.* After sitting at the bedsides of so many terminally ill people, I can't understand a God who would work that way. It just doesn't make sense.

Although I did it for so many years, I can no longer rationalize unanswered prayer. I can't deny reality any longer.

Looking back over the course of my life, I would not say that God never answered my prayers or spoke to me. If I'm honest, I feel confident saying that four or five of those times I thought I heard God speak or saw a prayer answered, I'm pretty sure it was God. It's pretty humbling to think that I expected to hear from him and to have him guide every step of every day; I can only wonder at the arrogance in that certainty, the arrogance that I thought I had figured out the inscrutable Creator of the universe and that I was chosen above others to receive his blessings.

Still, when I look back on that day in Denver when I prayed to find my cousin Brad, I want to believe that God intervened. I want to believe that God really did smile on me, that he really did have my path cross with my cousin's. But I still can't say for certain, and I think if I tried to, I'd wonder why he'd answer something so silly and yet ignore the prayers I prayed for Cheryl.

That line of thinking would only lead to more questions, and more struggling against a reality that I could not change then and cannot change now. Acceptance seems to be one of the biggest lessons I have learned throughout this process: to accept what is in life instead of insisting on something else.

I saw a woman in the hospice care center recently who used to go to my church. She is incredibly sick with cancer, and the doctors have recommended stopping treatment because it is so advanced. Yet she believes, as I believed and Cheryl believed and so many others believed, that God is going to step in and change the natural law and alter her course of life. She believes with everything she is that she will be magically healed.

I would never say that it won't happen, but her certainty brought back a flood of memories for me. I think about the high expectations I had for prayer, expectations that were so high that they were doomed to fail, and I can almost anticipate the pain and disappointment she will feel once she realizes that the cancer is a reality. I want nothing more than for her to be protected from that pain; I wish I could somehow use my experience to peel off the layers of the onion one at a time so that she could accept her situation and find comfort and peace in that space.

That may seem like resignation, but it's actually the only reasonable thing to do in the face of a cancer doctors say they cannot cure—prepare yourself that they might be right instead of living in denial. I see so much pain when people cannot accept the reality of their illness, the reality of their own mortality, the reality that miracles are not everyday occurrences given to anyone who asks or those who are "in" with God.

In my life, it seems a lot more appropriate to say that more often than not God does not intervene, rather than following some long, arduous train of thought that tries to rationalize why things happened the way they did. It makes more sense to say that he simply did not intervene with Cheryl's disease. Instead, the natural laws of earth were in place and stayed in place. Though I used to believe that God would intervene regularly and for any of his children who asked with enough faith and hope, now I accept that if God does act and does change the course of human history, it's the exception, not the rule.

I have so much peace now that I am not insisting that my life must be different than what it is. I don't really pray anymore, not in the way I used to. I don't ask God for things, and it's almost as if a complete reversal has occurred in my mind. Instead of sitting and waiting for God to make something happen in my life, I want to take the bull by the horns and do everything I can to make things happen for myself. I feel responsible for my own life and my own actions, and that gives me more confidence, self-assuredness, and satisfaction than I ever thought it would. I have found this a really healthy place to be, where I am not second-guessing God or myself.

This newfound responsibility has led me to a place where I can trust myself to do what I need to do, and if God needs to step in, he will. Sometimes I find myself in a conversation with a patient or a friend, and I sense that there is another presence there as I am speaking. It's a heightened awareness that impacts both of us, and I know what I am saying is touching them in a way that expresses love and compassion and gives them comfort during a difficult time. To me, that's a new type of communion with God, when I feel that he is with me as I counsel people who are hurting and grieving, who are seeking his grace.

Letting go of my old idea of prayer and working things out on my own has brought about another profound change.

And that is this: I no longer see the world in terms of what it is not giving me, but in terms of what it is. Instead of feeling that things are missing, I feel gratitude for what I have.

I make less money now than I did when I was the pastor at Canyon View, but I feel grateful that I can pay my mortgage. I have relatively few friends compared to the days when I was leading such a large church, when more people than I could handle were eager to be close to me, but I am so grateful for the quality of those relationships, for the loyalty those people have shown me, for the support those people give me, and the opportunities I have to try to repay their gift to me.

I feel gratitude as I sit on my patio in the morning where hummingbirds are sipping sugar water from my hummingbird feeder, and I watch the sun rise in a brilliant display of color, not with a list of things I need from God, but with a sense that I am blessed to simply be watching the sun rise again.

In that moment, I am overcome and want to praise the majestic Being that created such wonder and beauty. I can just say, "Thank you."

That's the most heartfelt prayer I've prayed in years—maybe the most heart-felt prayer I've uttered in my whole life.

CHAPTER 5

GOD IN HIS OWN IMAGE...OR MINE?

I have never doubted the existence of God.

Doubting would be unlikely after my Tuesday night experience as a child, an experience where I felt filled with what I can only describe as peace and comfort from a divine source, an experience I didn't ask for and one I have never really been able to explain.

Yet maybe if that had been the only time I had such an experience, I might have chalked it up as a fluke. Years later, I might have looked back on it as the overactive imagination of a child.

But it wasn't the only time. It happened again in January of 1971, when I was a young man training with Youth With A Mission in Lausanne, Switzerland. Cheryl and I were newly married, and even though I was in this training, I was really not completely back in the religious fold quite yet. I had spent the last couple years of high school acting out, and in college, I hadn't practiced or adhered to a religious faith in any meaningful way. As I said before, I had joined YWAM to see the world, not to be a missionary. But one evening during the School of Evangelism, we had a lecture (like we did every evening), and it did something to me. Though like my first encounter all those years before I can't remember what the topic of the talk was, I left that lecture and something moved in my heart.

Cheryl and I lived in room 17 in the Hotel du Golf, YWAM's first campus. In my mind, I can go back to that room in Lausanne, to our small apartment, and to the bathroom where I secluded myself in the midst of our busy community. As I sat there in that quiet, somehow I knew I was encountering God again, sensing that same presence I had as a kid. Despite the fact that I had been rebelling against my inherited worldview for several years and had mostly stepped away from my faith, I didn't feel any judgment in that moment. There wasn't a bony finger pointing at me, condemning my faults and my mistakes. Instead, I sensed that the past had been settled, that it had probably always been settled, and I just knew that I was okay. The funny thing was, I hadn't prayed a prayer of repentance; I hadn't asked Jesus to come into my life. It was just that something happened. His grace descended upon me, and it was wonderful. Later, I told a friend that something had so lifted from me I felt like I could bounce.

I've always looked back at that experience and felt that, in that soothing, comforting space, I learned what it meant to be the prodigal son. I knew how it felt to experience God the first time as a child and—despite all of the steps I had taken to move away from him, to shut him out along with my rigid childhood faith—to have him welcome me back. In fact, it was a sweeter experience the second time, partly because it was familiar, but also because of what Jesus says— when you are forgiven much, you love much. That second encounter made me feel endeared to God again. It's like a parent saying, "It's no big deal that you wrecked my car. I love you. I'm glad you're safe. We'll get it fixed." It made me feel like God *wanted* to redeem everything, and it still moves me.

So during my time with YWAM, I tried to share that amid the countercultural movement in Afghanistan and with soldiers we worked with in Germany, and I returned to Grand Junction with my mind set on the prodigal—on how I was the prodigal son, and that there were other prodigal sons and daughters who needed to find their home in this rich, loving, forgiving Father who had offered me so much peace.

Sadly, that experience was not the God who stayed at the forefront of my mind. Other images (ones I was taught, though I hadn't experienced) quickly crowded him out. God as the Father who would give me what I needed. God the protector who would save me from difficulties. God who knew every hair on my head and knit me in my mother's womb, whose blessings proved I was important. God who was almighty and powerful, who it helped to have on my side and whose wrath it was dangerous to attract. God who had set down laws, was inflexible, and had to be obeyed.

Those were the images of the God I believed in until all the images and the promises and the certainties failed me, and I had to get back to the essence.

I've spoken already about how I prayed for answers and how I felt God ignored them. But I'm going to speak about it a little more to show how buying into ideas about God that were different from my experience of him left me devastated and broken.

You see, I heard many people tell me over the years who God was, even though I'd already had two pivotal experiences that showed me. Instead of leaning into what I knew to be true—that God was love, that he was that peace and lightness I felt in those two mystical encounters—I listened to what other people said about him.

In one way, my deference to other people on who God is doesn't quite make sense. I had an experience with God where he did not condemn me, where he did not make me feel ashamed, yet I let other people tell me that's what God would do.

I had an experience with God where he did not give me anything but a sense of calm presence, but I expected he would give me anything I wanted, both material and spiritual, because some teacher along the way had pulled a verse from the Bible and hammered it into my head.

But then again, believing what other people told me about God instead of trusting my own experience was in keeping with my upbringing. I was taught to obey authority, not to question, and to believe believe believe.

As a child, I was taught that God was harsh on those who were outside the fold, but for those inside, he was going to feed you every day. He would give you manna. He would be your provider and shelter, and in the face of the alternative—the God who would condemn someone to hell for unbelief—the provider God was the better end of the deal. If I look back honestly, I can say I believed in those images of God not only because it was the only option, but also because I would benefit if he really were that way.

Then in YWAM, it got even more personal. I was taught that I would hear frequent words from God and see frequent signs from him that would guide my life. One teacher in particular taught about the infallibility of prayer and that we would hear from God daily. It was an exciting idea: that I would have frequent and undeniable communication with the all-powerful and all-knowing Creator of the universe. It made me feel important, significant, and powerful in a world that often makes us feel unimportant, insignificant, and powerless.

I believed—and I probably said this hundreds of times over the years—that we gravitate to God because we need God. It makes sense. If he has everything and tells you, "Ask of me," then if you have a need, you ask and expect an answer. You may be asking for something medical science can't give you, or something you can't provide for your loved one. Who else would you turn to in your hour of need? Who else but the almighty Father could answer you?

Unsurprisingly, I was at a loss when my experience contradicted those images, when I called out to him and the only response I experienced was a resounding and almost palpable silence. Actually, "at a loss" isn't the most accurate way to describe it. I had believed and taught about this God who would never let me down. His silence was crushing.

With all the problems I was facing, problems that became heavier the longer they stayed around, problems that needed solutions that human beings couldn't supply, I thought God's intervention was inevitable. At my lowest points, when the church was unmanageable and my marriage was wrecked and everything I did left me feeling depleted and despairing, I can remember crying out to God with all the sincerity I could muster—"Do anything, but don't be silent! Tell me something good or bad, or just tell me 'I'm too busy with others right now.'"

These weren't just thoughts that came into my mind. They were words that came to my lips, often involuntarily. I remember going out into the mountains and desert places by myself and feeling so much despair and loneliness that I literally yelled out to him and heard my words disappear into the silence around me. "Where are you?" I cried. "Say something! Do something! Just don't make me feel so abandoned, so alone, so completely by myself!"

Days later, nothing would have happened. Nothing changed, and I could sense nothing but silence and absence. I followed the rules and professed the beliefs of the church, hoping God's mystical presence would return, hoping he would answer my prayers. The silence and absence began wreaking havoc on everything I believed—the whole foundation of my life, which was centered around this image of God as someone who knew and loved me, who valued my service to him, who would intervene in my life when I needed him. In my mind, this question was always with me: *Where are you?*

It felt like abandonment. As I write these words, I can still feel the weight on my chest from that period of time, which in hindsight was the pain of a broken heart. During that time, I learned the difference between stillness and silence. In stillness, there is still presence. But the silence was a void, an abyss, a total absence, and it was unbearable.

I said early on that I was not disillusioned with God, but with myself. It has taken me a long time to realize that I was struggling with myself in that silence—that I had an imperfect image of who God was, and that I didn't truly know him.

What I had been taught and was teaching to others was just so starkly different from what I was experiencing, and that gap became too big to countenance. Finally, I came to the same conclusion about God that I did about the rules and regulations of the church: *that my experience was stronger than my theology.*

And that's where I have stayed. At this point, what I experience in my daily life is far more influential than all things I learned from others and then taught to my congregations for my entire life. When my faith fell around me, I needed a new understanding of God, to expand that space for him in my mind and in my spirit, to reassess what his expectations of me were and what I could expect from him.

In doing this, I've stepped away from the idyll of God as a kind grandfather in the sky who can give me anything I want. Instead, I have developed a pragmatic faith based on a combination of my tempered hopes about who God is and who I have experienced him to be.

But this was a process, like peeling back the layers of the onion, getting closer and closer to the truth that God wasn't who I had been told he was, but that he was something completely different that I would have to find out on my own. This was when I began looking for examples of others who have gone through this, and of course, I came across Mother Teresa. In her letters, published after her death, she reveals that after an early life with an intense connection with the divine, she didn't feel the love of Christ for almost forty years.

This calls to mind the darkest of the psalms, like Psalm 22. "My God, my God, why have you abandoned me?"

Or Psalm 13. "How long, Lord?" the psalmist cries. "Will you utterly forget me? How long must I carry sorrow in my soul, grief in my heart day after day?"

Or the one that echoes from the bottom of the abyss, Psalm 88. "But I cry to you for help, Lord; in the morning my prayer comes before you. Why, Lord, do you reject me and hide your face from me?" The last line plumbs the depths: "My only friend is darkness."

There are so many examples both in the Bible and in life where people are not hearing from God on a daily basis, so many times that they beg for God to respond. These laments are heartfelt entreaties that ask God to show his mercy. "Don't hide your face!" they plead. "Please hear me! Don't turn away from me when I need you! Do not be deaf to my cries!"

In my mind, any theology that tries to gloss over this silence will inevitably face a reality check. Preachers who tell their congregations they will hear from God every day will end up being proven wrong. Many of the Christians who believe beyond any doubt that God will answer their prayers for miraculous intervention will be disappointed.

Because even the children of Israel went 432 years without hearing the voice of God, before Moses came to lead them from their trials in Egypt.

I wonder about so many things now.

Like how many times God really did answer my prayers. Was he a present and guiding force in building the church, or was it human effort that brought Canyon View Vineyard its successes? Did Cheryl really receive miraculous healing, or was that ten-year reprieve just the way MS works?

Like how many times it was actually God when I said I heard his voice. How many times was it me—how many times did I hear what I wanted, how many times did I see what I wanted? I remember sitting behind my desk at Canyon View and giving someone a "word," and I cringe to think that many of those times, maybe I just made it up.

From where I am now, it also surprises me that I was so flippant, declaring who God was and what I expected he would say to me and do for me. Between my belief that God was my personal miracle worker and my mystical encounters with him, I think I developed a sort of spiritual pride, and I felt qualified to invoke his name to support whatever advice I was giving or whatever decision I wanted to make.

I was not the only one. Over the years, I don't know how many times I'd watch people become romantically involved, and then one of them would get a word from God that they weren't supposed to get married. The only thing I am certain of in that situation is that the person who uses God as a breakup tool is too cowardly to take responsibility for a difficult decision, so he or she blames it on God to end the discussion.

Or God was used in the event of a possible move to another city, or a new job opportunity, or any major life decision that requires serious consideration. Believers invoke God's name and his voice in almost every conversation you can imagine, and when that happens, there's not much you can say back. In essence, it's a power play. We toss God around like it's a game.

But if you look in the Bible at when God speaks, *huge things happen.* God spoke and the world came into existence. God spoke and a dove came down from heaven to announce Jesus as Savior. But we just throw his name around for anything, trivial or profound.

I don't mean to say that God never speaks. I think over the years, I had a few true impressions from God. But the number of times could probably fit on one hand, and I've spent a lot of time asking for his word. Looking back, I think I wanted things to be from God, so I made myself believe they were. That's what people do. It's almost a catch-22, because people are waiting on you to hear from God, and so you come up with *something,* as if you are Moses and God speaks with you face-to-face, every day.

In a recent conversation, a woman was explaining something she was going through, and it was like she was speaking to me about my own life. What she said to me was profound because it gave me direction about what I needed to accomplish in my life. It was one of those moments that seemed sacred. Does God guide us or speak to us? I believe he does. And I believe his guidance comes in many different forms.

But the certainty that God is pointing me in one way, or that he is giving a decisive answer, has left me. I would rather sit with that still, small voice than convince myself it is directing me somewhere. And the still, small voice does come to me. I have confidence that the rush—not what happens from the outside in, but from the inside out, whether it's through a song, a book I'm reading, or someone speaking to me, or when I'm in nature and I sense that presence—that's God.

Where is the presence of God in my life? It's not in the big, big things that God does, because normally he doesn't do that. A miracle, by its very definition, is the suspension of natural law. What if someone stepped off a cliff, and God suspended gravity? A lot of people would be floating around. So the miracle is the rarity. If God granted miracles to everybody all the time, there would be no common rule, no certainty or predictability in our world. He can't work miracles for everybody, or two plus two would not equal four.

Despite losing my ideas about God as a literal friend, as a literal father, as a literal provider of both the mundane and the miraculous, something still pulls me toward belief.

It's just not the belief I had before. Because if I look at what happened to

Cheryl and think God healed her for ten years, I am left wondering why he would take that away. That kind of suffering and the suffering I see around me at hospice brings up so many questions. I see people who served God their whole lives, and they endure painful and prolonged deaths incongruous with the lives they've led. I see my mother, who at eighty-six was still attending prayer meetings at her church until she fell recently and broke her pelvis. Now she's immobile and in pain, waiting to die but unable to. If there was ever a good reason for someone to die, it's someone who is in pain and asking to die because they don't have any quality of life.

I can't reconcile the vast suffering on this planet with the God I was taught about as a child and a young man. I have studied all of it—free will, the influence of evil, the goodness that God hopes for us—and it simply doesn't make sense. I can look over at my library and see four or five books about suffering that I've read, just trying to figure this whole thing out. None can explain it to me. In fact, the more I look at it, the further the answer moves away. Instead of answers, I end up with more questions.

To some extent, working in hospice perpetuates this. I see the pain and the agony on people's faces, and I hear family members telling me, "I just can't do this one more day" as their loved one hangs on and hangs on and hangs on. They have prayed. They've told their loved one—as if this is some sort of magic that will break the spell—that it's okay for them to go, as if that is going to get them over the edge. But really, I don't see that it has any effect. The pain of death is just one of those things that people have to endure.

To those who would say, "It all happens for a reason"—the old Christian cliché that tries to rationalize the confusion, the anger, and the utter morass of human suffering—I just have to throw up my hands. Because yes, there are some attempts to explain suffering and God's role in it in Scripture. In Romans 11:22, Paul writes about the paradox, the kindness and the severity of God. That word *severity* very aptly describes Sodom and Gomorrah. Or the great flood. Or the story of Uzzah, the Levite. His story is particularly devastating. When the ark of the covenant was stolen by the Philistines, they built a cart to carry it and put oxen in front of it. But when they began to move it, the oxen stumbled and Uzzah stuck his hand out and steadied the ark. Immediately, God killed him. Even before my disillusionment, I read that and I thought, "No. He couldn't have. He couldn't have." Uzzah was just trying to help. It's bizarre—the idea that that object was more sacred than the life God created. And I say to myself, *If this is who God is, and this is how he deals with humans, then I don't want to know him.* I can't love a God who would send that kind of suffering, whether it is for punishment or for the person's greater good. Because that type of suffering destroys people.

Yet I understand the hold that theology can have on someone's mind, and how they have trouble unlearning these ideas about God. I was trained that God was that way, and it was difficult to let go of. Only recently, a friend took me out to lunch, and as I was pondering the weight of what I have been through, she said to me, "Don't believe in a God who punishes you for your actions." Big tears came into her eyes as she said it again. "Don't believe that."

Now that I am faced with sickness and death on a daily basis, I find that I really can't escape this spiritual journey. I have to keep moving forward to get to the core of who God is; I can't just fall back into what I know and repeat the old Christian clichés. In hospice, sometimes patients or their family members do, and it gives them comfort, and I just let them talk.

But other times they are struggling with questions, questions about God and suffering and death. And I tell them, "David was really mad at God. And if it was okay for David to be mad at God, it's okay for you to be mad at God." At that level, I am connecting. I don't have the answers, but I try to help them get to the heart of their pain.

Once they air their frustrations and I don't give them oversimplified answers, they actually do feel better. Somehow, that just breaks something open inside— both for patients and for families. They're able to say, "I just don't understand this." Interestingly, I find I build connections with these fellow sojourners exactly because I am not trying to slap a Band-Aid on a festering wound. To them, I am in exactly the same position—"I am just like you."

I think this is the process I have to go through to reconcile myself to God, a process that just has to unfold as it unfolds. In some ways, this is a long death, a death that has to occur before my faith can be resurrected. If that means I walk in the desert for a while, well, that's what I have to do. God took the Israelites into the desert to get Egypt to die in them. And my desert is this place of search-ing, of being not quite sure I have all the answers, so that part of me that had it all figured out—my Egypt—can die.

And yet, I am confident that some things won't pass away. After all the suf-fering I have seen in my life, I still gravitate toward belief in God, and I still cling to the hope that he is my friend. The Bible doesn't prove there is a God; it assumes there is a God. And that assumption gives me peace. It gives me peace to think there is someone who ordered and continues to order this world. Thinking there is no God does something to my hope. John Paul Sartre once said, "No finite point has meaning unless there is an infinite reference point." For me, that's true. If I am made in God's image, I have significance. If there is no God, I don't see any purpose. Nothing makes sense to me without him.

Now my spiritual journey is finding a new perspective of who God is and how I can live with him.

The last several years, I have been working this out. When I had my breakdown, the person I thought God was—the idea of him in my mind—crumbled. It started to unwind, and it kept unwinding until it got all the way to the core. There was no way to stop it. It was almost involuntary, as were the different emotions—anger, sadness, loneliness, confusion—that wracked me.

In those first days, weeks, and months, I still believed that God existed, but I had no idea what to believe *about* him. It was like I had cut the moorings loose from everything I believed—from the reliable institutions that supplied all my answers—and I knew I was floating away from the harbor that was so safe but where I would waste away if I stayed any longer.

So several months in, I started this journey of working things out. I devoured books by Christians and non-Christians on both theological and practical matters, and I began speaking to people who, like me, struggle with the orthodox answers. I lived, and I learned from that living. And from there, I began to rebuild a core of faith that centers on a gracious God.

That's the hope I cling to: that God is all grace.

I have such high hopes that he will redeem everything. Unlike the narrative of condemnation, the narrative of redemption makes sense to me. When I was raising my kids, spanking them was the hardest thing in the world. As a boss, I hated firing people. To be harsh with someone, even if I needed to be, was terribly difficult. But thinking that God is grace activates the side of my character I want to develop, helping me cultivate kindness and patience and all of the qualities I associate with grace. Those are the things that bring about forgiveness and rec-onciliation and healing, and in the end, peace.

So ultimately, that's my hope about his nature and his character: that God is the embodiment of all the things that bring peace. And I can spin in that orbit for a long time, just basking in the glory of that God.

In some ways, this image I have of God is quasi—it's half-formed. I don't have a list of God's names or his characteristics that I have dug from Scripture. I don't have a theological treatise that explains his exact nature and how he consistently manifests himself throughout time.

Because honestly, I don't understand every expression of God's character that appears in Scripture. In fact, I hate some of the images of God in Scripture. And what am I supposed to do with that?

I have to go back to my experience, to my reality. I have to realize that those images of God are somebody else's, and I brush them to the side, saying to myself, "Well, that hasn't been true for me."

One of those descriptions, one that used to give me so much hope but now just makes me feel confused, was the description of God as faithful. Some people might think that I'm being a "cafeteria Christian," or worse, blasphemous when I say that I don't know if God is faithful, but I can't deny what I experienced. The times I cried out, he was silent; and I struggle with that. I still struggle as I watch families in hospice crying out as their loved ones are dying, as they come to the realization that, even though they have been told that he will, God is not going to change their reality. So what I mean to say is that God was not faithful in the way I interpreted those passages or in the way we all spoke about and believed. To say otherwise is a rationalization that borders on denial.

In some ways, I can understand when people don't accept the reality that they are encountering. It's too much. Throughout my previous faith life, there were doubts that would come up, and I would say immediately, "I can't think this stuff." My doubts were about doctrines that had been around for centuries and millennia, and under that weight, I felt I had to push those thoughts down and say to myself, "No, that's not a question I can ask." Instead of really struggling with my questions, I denied them because I didn't know how to work out the contradictions.

I am not alone in this. I know a lot of people who will not admit their expectations of God have failed them. They just can't go there. They believe that he has a reason for not intervening, that there is a purpose in it. And now I look at that denial and I say, "Oh, God. Help us to be honest more than anything."

Jesus faced this! He cried out, *"My God, my God, where are you?"*

Of course, it's not just worrying about being blasphemous that makes that admission—that God has failed them—difficult. When I finally admitted it, I was coming from a place where I believed God was a protector and was going to buffer me from trouble. Without that belief, I felt so vulnerable, lost, and alone.

But I don't feel that way anymore. Now, I feel like am in control of my life and more responsible for myself. When something goes wrong, I don't ask, "Why isn't God doing anything?" Instead, I ask, "What did I do wrong, and what can I do next time to prevent this from happening?"

To me, it's liberating. My reality and my theology aren't so far apart that between them is a rubber band about to snap. Now, I have predictable and reasonable expectations for the world. I can accept the fact that the only behavior I can change is my own, and that I can't force God's hand. And my desire to do so is gone. One of my favorite Bible verses used to be John 15:5—"I am the vine and you are the branches; apart from me, you can do nothing." I loved the idea that we had this strength on our side, that Jesus would give us life and help us through anything, that God was going to come through. On a basic level, I do believe that we are the branches and that he is the vine—that he is our eternal source, the place from which we came and the spring of life that animates us. But I realize that in my former spiritual life, I took those words too literally. Now I believe that we have to live our lives on our own.

A big part of that is realizing that the answers aren't simple. In Promise Keepers, they would say, "God is good." And the expected response was, "All the time." I can't see it that simplistically anymore. This summer I was talking to a friend about God, and she said, "He is the God of life." And I thought, *He is also the God of death.* It's hard to even say it: to admit the dark side of God. It's unnerving. But what is the final judgment if not darkness? When it comes down to it, why would a loving God want his last act in human history to be judgment? Why would he want that? I remember watching the movie *In Cold Blood* and thinking, *How can one human being sentence another human being to death?* And for God to do that to billions of people? If it's true that God will do this, that's a dark side. That won't be a happy day.

I've come to accept that there are elements of darkness and light in this world, and that I don't perfectly understand the Creator. It goes back to Paul: "We all see through a glass darkly." None of us get it. I can't hold to that black-and-white thinking anymore and pretend that I do. I can only find comfort in the gray area, of not quite knowing, of not quite being sure, but hoping for grace and mercy.

I still gravitate toward the idea that God is eternal and that he brought this world into existence and us with it. Years ago, I encountered some teachings on this subject that were formative and have really stuck with me, teachings by Winkie Pratney, a great Christian thinker, who used energy on an atomic level to question how something so marvelous could have developed without God saying "Let there be"; by Charles Finney, teaching about how humans cannot fathom the universe without a first cause; and a teaching by Francis Schaeffer, who said that it is not hard for us to think of the infinite in the future, but to think that there was never a beginning is beyond our imagining. These things confound our minds, and to me, that inscrutability is God.

But other things are less certain and more of a hope, a joyful expectation that God is all of the things that bring me peace. I pray and hope that he is kind and merciful and gracious and long-suffering. In the Psalms, God says, "I remember you are but dust." He knows where we are as humans, that we are broken. He understands that we are not going to be perfect. That's the message of redemption.

And very intensely, I believe in the God I've experienced. In recent years, I've been visited by a stillness and peace that I believe is divine presence. It happens at various times, intermittently—out on my Harley, up in the mountains, out fishing. Those encounters reinforce my desire and my belief. I don't expect that presence, and it's not continuous, it's not every time, but when it does happen, it's like, *This is God*. In those moments I am enjoying myself, and it seems like there's a reciprocal effect from the universe that I was made to enjoy these moments, moments where I think, *The world is right*. Everything seems to make sense. I wish that I could live there, but instead, those are special occasions. I say, if heaven is like this, then yes.

I want that experience of God, that peace, that presence, that solace, as do half the American population, who attest to the fact that they have had some type of mystical experience.[3] People want the warmth and comfort and peace of a higher power. They want to believe their souls matter, that the miraculous exists. But they don't want the judgment, the rigidity, and the hypocrisy that exist in our institutions. They don't want to be a part of hateful rhetoric that condemns people to hell.

And I don't either. Probably one of the most important illusions I lost was that I was more beloved, more important, and closer to God than other people.

His silence disabused me of the notion that I was a favorite. Instead, I learned that I was only one of his many beloved, who at this point number seven billion. I learned that God doesn't have favorites; he loves his children equally.

So my disillusionment has been a great equalizer. Now, I don't make assumptions about other people—about their religious upbringings or their lifestyles. One thing I am pretty certain of is that I don't have any more special access to God than the Buddhist in Tibet. In my heart, I used to harbor belief that people who weren't living a Christian lifestyle couldn't be enjoying their lives, but I was wrong. I'm relieved to be free of that prejudice and judgment. When people say they are agnostic or atheist, my first reaction isn't to try to convince them of something else or to show them the "right" way. Now, I listen.

Because I have let go of that judgment, I find that I see God as much more lenient, much more relaxed. He gets it—he gets who I am. And I think he'd much rather I be who I am than who I was trying to be back then. He's authentic, and the more authentic I become, not only in myself, but in who I think he is, the better our relationship grows. I can say these things without the fear of punishment. For me, *that's huge*—to think, *He loves me, and he doesn't want to send me to hell.*

In fact, I think he is proud that I am trying to work this all out. He probably even knows I might never get it all straight, but he appreciates that I'm being honest, as honest as I ever have been in my life about how I feel and how I think.

But I still I can't go to church, at least not to any of the churches I have been to. Because this one-size-fits-all idea—in religion, if you buy the package, you get the good, the bad, and the ugly—I can't tolerate anymore. I can't search things out in a sharp-edged space where I am being judged on every word. And it's undeniable that judgment is all over the walls of Christendom. Recently, I saw an old teacher of mine who went to the same church I was raised in come out of the City Market, a grocery store in town. Instead of greeting me with kindness and recognition of our common humanity, he looked at me and quickly turned his head to pretend he didn't see me. And I thought, *That's what I cannot bear—* that self-righteous arrogance that says, "We've got it all figured out, and you don't."

Yet people outside those circles who I am friends with now, they just love me. They don't care what I did. That's the kind of love Jesus talked about. He was the friend of sinners, and he loved unconditionally. This is a better expression of who God is to me now.

Now, I see God reflected through people like my friend Val. Recently, the mother of one of my coworkers passed away, and Val was the first one who stepped in to offer her condolences, comfort, and aid. Val also does things for her patients all the time, and she never talks about it—talk about your left hand not knowing what your right is doing. Val would not call herself a Christian, but to me, she exhibits the best expressions of love and kindness I've ever seen.

I see so many people like her who are sharing love—disinterested, unconditional love—who weren't taught love in the Christian way. I experience God through all kinds of people, people I might disagree with philosophically or theologically but who don't constantly manifest that jagged edge of judgment and that threat of rejection. There's a sense that God is there and working with them and through them, and I have no sense of responsibility to change them or make them into somebody I want them to be.

And I have faith that because he is working in these people, he is reconciling them to himself. Again, this is without our knowledge or permission, and it tells me that he reconciles and redeems and showers his love and his grace upon people regardless of who they are, what they believe, or what lifestyle they choose to lead.

In essence, this is the message of redemption, and it is so much more moving than the story of judgment, and I revel in that. I bask in that warmth, thinking, *This is God's feeling toward everybody. We're not that far from God—any of us.* I revel in the idea of God as grace, that God is all of the things that bring salvation and liberation: being authentic, honest, loving, forbearing, nonjudgmental, and accepting. Those things seem undeniably *good,* and they seem like who God is. He's the God who wants to love everyone, and he is the God who wants to show his mercy to everyone. This is the God I can love, the one who has always pulled me toward himself. Even if people don't want to be with him, he's gracious enough to give them that space until they eventually see who he is. I love that image of God, the one who tells me that that nobody is beyond his mercy, nobody is beyond his grace.

The experiences I have now support and reinforce that God, and because I experience him in my life, I can live with this. My reality does not contradict my theology; my reality now reinforces my theology.

And at the bottom of all of this, at the core of my new faith and my new idea of God, is my faith and hope and trust that God is long-suffering. It's trust that God isn't going to send me to hell because I'm trying to work through all this and discover who he is using my own conscience, my own experience, my own common sense, and my own hope.

That's the heart of what I have learned and what I want to share with people. The core of what I want to say is this:

It's okay that you have to start all over again. Because what you thought about God and church and salvation and all of that just didn't work. When you've decided you can no longer be pulled by that chain, it's okay. You are safe asking these questions.

When nothing makes sense, and you are lonely, confused, and afraid, it's okay. You can take the time to search and find God, and you can meander down the paths you need to in order to find truth and light and peace and an authentic faith that is your own. God's shoulders are big enough to handle your questions, and he has grace enough for all of it.

And eventually, you will find out who God is, and when you do, you're going to live in that sphere, spin in that orbit, bask in that glow.

The thing is, that one might break down too, and the process will start again, but again, you'll find out who he is. He will lead you there.

CHAPTER 6

THE BIBLE

About fifteen years ago, I met another pastor, a man who was a close friend, for lunch at a McDonald's. From this far distance, I can remember what should have been a forgotten midday meal with striking clarity. The distinctness of the memory is not because of what happened that day in history or who we saw there, certainly not because of the burgers we ate, and not because of a significant personal event or a pressing local issue.

It's because I sat down with him, and in a hushed and confidential tone, I asked him a question that confessed so much.

Have you ever questioned the inerrancy of the Word?

Of course, before I asked it, I made him promise he'd never share my question with anyone, which he answered with an unequivocal "yes." Then came my question, and as he heard it, he sat there shocked for a moment, his face a mixture of stunned and relieved and guilty. I knew at that second he'd had exactly the same questions, but he had also been afraid to talk about it.

After a minute, he confirmed my suspicions.

"Yes. I have," he said heavily.

And he began his litany of uncertainties.

We sat there for hours, airing our doubts, sharing our consternation. It's hard to overstate how antithetical this seemingly harmless conversation was to our belief systems. We were fundamentalists; our doctrine was that every word of the Bible was God-breathed, and therefore, perfect.

I was taught, and I taught my congregations, that if any of the Bible was false, then all of it is false, but I found myself confessing that I was hung up on things like whether or not David actually had exactly five stones in his shepherd's bag when he fought Goliath. How are we sure that detail is right? I asked him. The story had been told for many years before it was written down, and recopied and translated countless times after that. What if a human had erred?

At the time, I was so all-or-nothing that my next question was this: if I doubted the five stones, how could I believe John 3:16? This may seem like a trivial worry, but for me it was pivotal. The Bible was the infallible, inerrant Word of God. It was my certainty, my guide to life, my proof of God's favor and blessing and interest in me. And I can remember that as I aired these questions, I was enormously afraid—afraid that I had bought into something that was false, afraid that I was going to lead hundreds of people into the same trap.

Yet despite my fear, speaking to my friend that day was healing. I left feeling like I was not alone in this conundrum, that I was not alone in my doubts about this integral pillar of the faith. Before this conversation, I had felt alone. I had never spoken of my doubts before, not to Cheryl or any other friend or colleague or family member. It was something I harbored secretly, because to be asking that question—*Is the Bible truly the inerrant Word of God?*—was tantamount to blasphemy.

Of course, that was as far as the conversation went. I didn't speak of it again for many years. The questions were there, and they were not going away, but for a long time, I just pushed down this struggle. I repressed it. Maybe that's because that's all I could handle at that point.

And what else could I do? I believed I had to be careful about what I let my mind dwell on. If I really started wrestling with my doubts, if I really started indulging that line of questioning, I knew I couldn't keep it to myself. I knew that I would begin to reveal it in my interactions with my friends and family, in my sermons.

Because out of the abundance of the heart, the mouth speaks.

Of course, today, I can handle the questions. And I can speak my heart and my conscience without fear.

Because who cares if there were fives stones or four? What matters is that a young shepherd boy with a few rocks and a leather sling killed a Philistine champion and proclaimed the glory of God.

I was in awe of the Bible as a child. My mom had a book of Bible stories for children that she used to read to me every morning. Many of us encountered these in our childhood, and the stories occupy seminal spaces in our minds. When I recall the Bible's significance in my earliest days, immediately my mind returns to our old house, and I am sitting by my mother as she reads me the story of Samson. I remember being enthralled by the story of the strong hero and his failures and victories. Whether or not I knew it was the Bible, I am not sure. I just knew it was compelling, and I loved it.

Of course, no one can maintain that simple response to such a complex text as the Bible through adolescence and adulthood. But we are asked to. I was taught that we were to accept the Bible in total, as a whole, without any question. As I explained earlier, it went like this: "If you don't believe one thing, you can't believe any of it."

In many ways, the Bible had the status of God in every faith tradition I was a part of—in my childhood church, in YWAM, at my own churches. It was the fourth person of the Trinity. John Wimber, the founder of the Vineyard Movement, used to complain that we have God the Father, God the Son, God the Holy Spirit, and God the Bible. We worship the Bible. And like you couldn't question the Father, you couldn't question the Word.

As a young man, this requirement not to question became more difficult to keep. In school, I started learning about dinosaurs that roamed the earth millions of years ago, and I couldn't figure out where they fit in the Bible. But because I couldn't ask the questions (which meant I couldn't find answers), I was silenced. My conscious mind, which had been trained by these religious figures, automatically began to shut those questions down because God forbid you would wade into those quandaries.

Through YWAM and adulthood, I found a way to repress those questions and reaffirm my commitment to the Word of God. Part of that was that in YWAM, we were filled with the enthusiasm of searching out what we thought were new and cutting-edge practices with the Bible—efforts to prove the existence of God using Scripture, efforts that appropriated the steps of the scientific method to prove our belief was valid. It felt so certain, and so important, since we were trying to justify an intellectual position for those people we were trying to evangelize.

Of course, proving the existence of God using the Bible was impossible, as the Bible *assumes* God exists but in no way proves it empirically. But that enthusiasm was enough to circle me back to where I began: to a hard and fast belief that the Bible was the inerrant Word of God, the guide to all of life's questions. Because not believing that was not an option, no one was going to convince me otherwise.

So beginning with YWAM and continuing for almost four decades, I read the Bible every day. I read it to be inspired. I read it for answers. I read it to discover a message to share with my church each Sunday. I was immersed in the Word, and I read and reread and memorized and recited those lines as if they were the panacea for all life's problems.

But there were times it was difficult to do it. There were times I dreaded opening the Good Book and trying to find one verse that would inspire me among the many. This was something I often kept to myself, but I remember speaking it aloud at least one time to a group of people. It was years ago, around the time I spoke to my friend at the McDonald's, when our church was still located at the old Chrysler Cathedral. Among a group, I said very bluntly, "Sometimes I read this book, and it's like sawdust."

I was trying to say that sometimes, the Bible alone didn't feed me. Sometimes it felt like it was speaking to another world (and indeed it was!). I was trying to say that sometimes, in the middle of reading Leviticus, you just want to throw up your hands and say, "Enough!"

I was looking at an older woman's face at that moment, an older woman who was the mother of my close friend and who was visiting our church from out of town. As soon as the word "sawdust" escaped my lips, I saw her face flush with shock, as if I had taken the Lord's name in vain in the pulpit.

I believe her reaction confirms John Wimber's point: we worship the Bible. I think her reaction speaks to the fact that many Christians put the Bible on a pedestal next to the Father, the Son, and the Holy Spirit, and we act like any time we feel confused or angry or frustrated or suspicious or just plain bored with the Scripture, it is some fault of ours and it's somehow condemnable.

So we mask our true feelings and our honest responses to keep from being condemned.

But I can say it now: I often felt bored by the Bible.

I can also say that I was confused by the Bible.

I can also say that I was suspicious of the Bible.

I can also say that I was hurt by the Bible, when the promises it made did not come through.

I can say those things without feeling guilty or worrying that someone is going to tell me that I'm on the road to hell. Because I no longer believe that I have to take every word of the Bible as undeniable fact, as literal truth. I do not reject the Bible; I still believe it is filled with timeless truths that can guide our paths as humans. But I do not believe I will be condemned by God for my questions.

And I have had many of them, and I have had them for decades. Like why was I still hungry for other words when I had the Bible at my fingertips? Why was I reaching for books written by my contemporaries to help me connect with God? Often the books would be expounding biblical themes or explaining some mystery, like the Holy Spirit. But instead of seeking those things out in the Bible, I would gravitate to modern authors because they were speaking to me in a contemporary way about how to communicate the gospel in late twentieth-century America. And there, instead of sawdust, I was finding sustenance. I used these books as a way to see the Bible in new ways that spoke to our contemporary condition as humans.

As time passed, I bought more and more of these books. I read everything I could get my hands on, and I was like a sponge. And when I thought I needed something more, I would go to the bookstore, pick something off the shelf, and read it. I'd let myself gravitate toward whatever looked the most appealing, whatever I was hungry for. Those shelves were like a buffet of food I never tired of.

It was a contrast to the Bible, which, at times, was tedium. Which, many times, confused me. A handful of times, I read the Bible in its entirety. I'd use one of those study guides that gave daily assignments, and I'd get through the entire Bible in a year. If I'm honest, it was something I did because it felt like an accomplishment. It was a goal I could set and feel good about, and something that might boost my credibility in a way.

But something unexpected happened when I did this. Because I was being forced to read something I wouldn't otherwise have read, certain Scriptures would stand out to me that didn't fit my paradigm. When I would see something in the Scripture in a new light or with new eyes, I would realize that it was changing my paradigm about either who I thought God was or what I thought the church was. Reading the Bible through allowed me to see the parts that I wouldn't have seen, that I might have resisted, that I certainly didn't understand. That I didn't know *how* to understand. And that was confusing.

At some points, instead of being simply confused, instead of being unsure of my ability to understand the Scripture, I was suspicious of the stories. I questioned the vindictive portrayals of God in the Old Testament. To this day, one particular story really sticks in my craw—when Joshua led the Israelites to war against the city of Jericho. It's a triumphant story, a story that would have been in that children's Bible that my mother read to me. When we're told that story, the trumpets blaring and walls falling are emphasized and the aftermath glossed over. But what happens after the walls collapse and everyone rushes in? We're told in the fifth chapter of the book of Joshua, in verse 21: "They devoted the city to the Lord and destroyed with the sword every living thing in it—men and women, young and old, cattle, sheep and donkey."

This passage has provoked different reactions in me. Sometimes I wonder whether this is truly God's nature. Could he really send a man to a city to raze it and wipe out every living inhabitant? But the other thought I've had is, *What if Joshua was wrong?* It was startling the first time I allowed myself to go there, to question whether or not that biblical father heard from God correctly. But who can believe beyond any doubt that these flawed humans could hear perfectly from God? Given the number of times I thought I heard from God, given the number of times I heard others talk about hearing from God, I'm not sure we can. It makes me suspicious of the phrase, and because of that, I am suspicious of these stories where humans use God as justification to do what they want to do, things like war and murder that directly contradict the message we get from Jesus in the New Testament.

Of course, I would have been committing professional suicide to talk about this suspicion while I was still a pastor. I would have been chased right out the door if I had stood up and questioned whether Joshua truly heard from God. In some ways, I think I sat on these questions because my lack of theological credentials undercut my confidence. I didn't have a PhD, so I felt like I wasn't qualified to be making these assertions. And I don't ever remember one lecture, one talk, one sermon that focused on whether or not the Bible was inerrant in all my years with the Vineyard or at pastors' conferences or leadership summits. Instead, "If you don't believe one thing you can't believe any of it" was so strong that I abdicated my own judgment, my own response to the Scriptures, and instead repeated the party line: *The Bible is a guide to life, your daily bread. It's inerrant, it's all true, and if we don't understand it, or if we are bothered by it, or if we are bored to death when we are reading it, it's our fault as human beings.*

Toward the end, I still maintained this outwardly, but I was a bit of a hypocrite because I knew that my life was not lining up with what I had been promised in the Bible. When I was at my lowest, I had turned to God's promises for provision, for protection, for comfort. They were outlined in the Bible. Psalm 91 is one I

repeated over, and over, and over, and over again during those darkest days. In
my head, again and again, and aloud:

> Whoever dwells in the shelter of the Most High
>> will rest in the shadow of the Almighty.
> I will say of the Lord, "He is my refuge and my fortress,
>> my God, in whom I trust."

> Surely he will save you
>> from the fowler's snare
>> and from the deadly pestilence.
> He will cover you with his feathers,
>> and under his wings you will find refuge;
>> his faithfulness will be your shield and rampart.

It was a message that exhorted me to hope in his protection, that assured me
of it. And I did. I hoped with all my heart and soul in his answer:

> "Because he loves me," says the Lord, "I will rescue him;
>> I will protect him, for he acknowledges my name.
> He will call on me, and I will answer him;
>> I will be with him in trouble,
>> I will deliver him and honor him.
> With long life I will satisfy him
>> and show him my salvation."

I read that psalm when Cheryl was sick, when I was becoming more and
more overwhelmed at the church, and then when I had my breakdown, during
the year before I left the church. But it was during that year that I reached that
sickening, dark place that said, "God isn't going to do this. This darkness isn't
going to go away."

Even now, years later, if I read Psalm 91 or turn over those verses in my mind,
I feel the remnant of that pain, pain I still can't adequately put into words. I can't
explain the despair I felt when I realized that all of the things I had thrown myself
into, professing with my mouth and my mind and my heart that there was going
to be a strong tower, that God would protect and rescue me, weren't such easy,

uncomplicated truths. And it was heartbreaking to face it every day.

During that year after my breakdown, I was still pastoring the church, but I was so heartbroken that I didn't want to study the Bible. I didn't want to be around church. I didn't want to be around Cheryl. I didn't want to be around God. I didn't want to be around godly friends. But every week, I had to deliver a message. Each week, I'd rely on my years of experience giving sermons to cobble something together, but I knew that soon enough people would begin detecting that my passion was just gone.

Because of the gap between my experience and Psalm 91, I have a hard time returning to that place. If I go back there, I relive the sense of abandonment that I felt in the deepest part of my being, when that expectation that he was going to be there was disappointed. That belief unraveled, that certainty unraveled, and because of this, one of the most painful things for me to do to this day is to read the Bible. The very things that used to bring me comfort are the things that bring me the most pain.

So I don't really read the Bible anymore. I don't pick up its worn leather and peruse its familiar pages. In fact, my mother recently asked me if I had a smaller copy that she could use, since hers was becoming more difficult for her to carry. Without a thought, I gave her my Bible from my days as a pastor. I did it without any sense of sadness or regret. In fact, it felt good. It felt right.

Because I don't need to worship the Bible anymore.

I am not exactly sure where that worship came from. Maybe people started worshiping the Bible because it was the only concrete thing they had. It was the only tangible thing. It's in black and white, and they can grab on to it. They can point to it and say, "This is certain." It's a way they can take the *noumenal*—that which cannot be seen or touched or proven—and make it *phenomenal*—something they can observe. Maybe I did the same thing.

But when I left behind the need for certainty and the need for concrete answers, when I left behind my need for a systematic theology of the Bible, I was able embrace the ancient idea of religion, which was not a set of beliefs to profess nor a set of rules to follow.

For the word religion derives from Latin roots that mean *to bond, to reconnect*.

And I can still do that. I can still feel a connection to the Divine without reading the Bible every day, even if biblical inerrancy is no longer a hill I am going to die on, even if I never open the Good Book again.

I have not left the Bible entirely behind. Because the many verses I memorized over the years still sit in my head. They still live with me. And surprisingly enough, when I am speaking publicly, it's like an old well that I can draw on. Those Scriptures just come to the surface of my mind, and I can relay them. And I find that what rises to the surface is the kernel, the heart, the parts that have always resonated with me the most: like "God is love."

There is something to be said about this. The trivial details—the trees I used to mistake for the forest—have faded away. Instead, I can hold onto the bigger picture, to the timeless truths that teach me how to love, how to be compassionate, how to show mercy, and how to forgive. Even how to forgive myself.

And even for people who don't believe in the inerrancy of the Word, I still think the Bible is a powerful and invaluable tool. It is absolutely bursting with timeless truths. Most people today do not care about historical evidence or context. They are not interested in learning Greek or Hebrew in order to understand the nuance of each verse. They care about what is happening in their lives today. So if you can pull a timeless truth that will offer them comfort or support in what they are facing, then it becomes something useful to them. It just speaks.

For me, that's what the Bible is. Sometimes a Scripture will just come alive in that moment, and it will allow me to reconnect with God. It's a moment of revelation, and I just want to live there, though it may only last for that moment. I'm finally approaching the Bible in the way I tried to teach my congregation to: that it is a living book that gives manna for that day, that provides the guidance needed in the moment.

I don't think the Bible is the only place we can get that manna. I think God can send it however he wants. I think he can send it through a song on the radio or a person who offers the right advice at the right time.

That has led me to a new belief: that there is more to be said about the inspired Word of God than there is about the written Word of God. Look at Jesus—he was the *living* Word of God. And he would say, "You have heard it said of old, but I say unto you *this*." So it was relevant, it was timely, it was for that moment, and the idea that God speaks to people outside of the Scriptures makes sense to me. When Jesus was speaking, he was speaking new words, new spirit, and when he spoke those words, they were to the living beings around him, not to some scribe who wrote it into a text.

I believe God can still do the same to help us on this journey. I truly believe that you can be lifted and inspired, and that inspiration doesn't have to come from the Word of God. It comes from life, and those experiences in life that reconnect you to who God is. It comes from *your* life.

I think that when we are narrow in our focus, when we narrow the ways that God can show us wisdom and guidance, we can get stuck. We can feel bored and frustrated and confused. I can liken this to an earlier time, when we drove on dirt roads. Those roads were more vulnerable to the elements, and after a rain, the tires of a car would cut ruts into the road. Over time, those tracks would become so deep that you could let go of the steering wheel, and those tracks would just take you where you needed to go. In some ways, that was easy. You just let the road take you where you needed to go. But it was also limiting. There was only one place to go, and that was where the road had always led you. The same thing can happen with faith. Sometimes, we can stay in the tracks because it's easier than really exploring new paths God may be leading us down.

But those new paths can be exciting and expansive, and they can reveal God in surprising places. I have a friend who is an eye surgeon, and he went to a rural village in India to do some volunteer work. There, he met an Indian eye doctor who did half of his practice for free. Half of his patients received free eye care because they had no money to pay.

This was a surprising part of my friend's spiritual journey, a little side path that totally changed the way he thought about God and salvation and the way that humans are linked by God's love. Because as my friend explained to me, "That Hindu was speaking more to me about a Christian life than I, as a Christian, ever could say to him."

In my old spiritual life, I would have dismissed that thought out of hand. I would have said that if the Hindu man wasn't doing good in the name of Jesus, then it wasn't truly good. He wasn't acting from the directive of the Christian Bible, so God wouldn't recognize his work. But now, I am enlivened by the idea that God spreads his truth and love anywhere he wants, through anyone he wants, through any medium he chooses. Sometimes it's through the Bible, and sometimes it's not.

One thing I know is that I am no longer interested in such narrow tracks. I no longer believe the Bible is the end-all source of wisdom and life. I no longer feel compelled to stand by every word of it, even down to the number of stones in the young shepherd's bag.

And I believe that when we get to the next place, we'll see that what mattered was how we loved, and we'll all let out a sigh of relief commingled with regret, wondering why we worried about the details so much.

CHAPTER 7

ON MARRIAGE

The very first time I ever saw Cheryl, it was the first day of high school, and I can remember looking at her and thinking, *That's the most beautiful girl I've ever seen in my life.* But it wasn't until weeks later, at the end of football season, that I got up the nerve to ask her out.

Cheryl had also grown up in Grand Junction, and even though it was a small town and we had personal friends in common, we never met before high school. She had been a track-and-field athlete—and a good one—in elementary and middle school, and after we started dating, we realized that I had probably watched her run many times at the community track meets. We thought it was fun that we'd been places together before we even knew each other. In some small way, it made us feel like our love was supposed to be, which was only solidified by the fact that we experienced several breakups but couldn't stay away from each other. We had an unmistakable sense that we were really in love, and things grew from there.

As I saw it, Cheryl had all the attributes a man would ever want in a wife and a friend and a lover. She was gorgeous, had a quick wit and a boisterous laugh, and was incredibly intelligent, one of the smartest people I've ever been around in my life. For many of the years I spent with her, one of the thoughts that always went through my mind was what a lucky guy I was.

By the time we got married, we had been together for about five years. We got married at my childhood church in a traditional ceremony that was quite large—there were probably 350 to 400 people there as witnesses that day. I was twenty years old. Cheryl was twenty-one.

We were so young.

On that December day, we knew what we were doing was important, and we felt that it was right. We were taking the next step in life, the step that made us adults, and we took it as a responsibility that we would carry forever. When I said, "I do," I sincerely meant that I was committed to Cheryl until the day that one of us died.

We were so clueless as to what that would take.

Ten days later, we left for Lausanne, Switzerland, and began our mission of spreading the gospel that became the foundation of our lives and our relationship.

For twenty-five years, that partnership worked pretty well. We had our time overseas, then returned to Grand Junction and started a family. Our daughter Wendy was born in 1973, and our second child, Mary, came along a few years later. In 1982, our son Jon was born, and it felt like our family was complete. Other than spending 1977 in Switzerland with YWAM, we lived the whole time in Grand Junction.

While I sold cars and then transitioned into the pastorate, Cheryl was a traditional homemaker and mother (an arrangement we both wanted). We had busy lives, but we managed to pay the bills and raise the kids and build a church, and we felt that what we were doing was good and important. We also felt that we could overcome any trouble, that we could weather any storm with God's aid, that our marriage would always be supported by God's hand.

It's hard to say if, with the kids and the church filling our time, we were distracted from the structural weaknesses in our marriage, or if we willfully ignored the things that would prove to be our demise.

If I had to pinpoint when I first realized our marriage was in a bad place, I would probably point to about ten years before it ended. We spent most of those years as empty nesters, and as the years passed, our lives became nearly separate. We slept in different rooms because Cheryl's illness disturbed her sleep, and by extension, mine. But what began as a means for me to get a good night's rest became a source of relief from the constant conflict we experienced when we were together. And that was true for both of us. For those ten years I prayed, hoping that things would get better, that God would somehow ease our troubles and set us back on the right path.

Divorce was unthinkable and impossible for us, not only because we were a pastor and his wife, but also because from childhood, we had been taught that it was wrong. We didn't have divorces in our own families or in the families of the people we had grown up with. It was almost unheard of.

Throughout my time as a pastor, I heard all the sermons and talks about keeping the marriage first, but honestly—and this was a recurring theme in our lives—we thought we were invincible with God on our side.

Of course, left long enough, the little foxes eventually begin to spoil the vine. And there were various little foxes that got to work.

In hindsight, I can see many of my own issues. I had a hard time being honest and confronting problems. For a long time, I thought talking about problems was complaining. This was a product of childhood: if we ever had a problem we wanted to talk about, it was decried as complaining, especially by my father. And as my older sister will attest, there was absolutely no room for complaining in our home.

As I grew up, I learned to swallow what was bothering me, even if it was a legitimate concern. I also learned that if I had a problem, it was probably my own fault, since authority figures couldn't be questioned and were never wrong. I also learned to suppress things that didn't have an easy answer, because that did not fit within our worldview, where all the answers of life were easily discovered in the concordance of a Bible.

These characteristics were already set within me when we married. They were only compounded by Cheryl's personality, by the fact that she had such a quick wit and cutting sarcasm, and by the fact that she was determined to win arguments. As time went on and her illness affected her moods more and more, this only intensified. By the time she was diagnosed with delusional disorder in 2006, Cheryl was like a porcupine: if you got close, you were going to get stuck. So if I had an issue that I knew Cheryl did not want to hear about, I just avoided it, suppressed it. If I tried to speak, often the words stuck in my throat.

But it wasn't until around 2006, when things had been bad for over a decade and were essentially beyond repair, that we learned one of the biggest mistakes we had made was something we had thought was so right: beginning in the mid-eighties and through the time I resigned from Canyon View, we made our mission of spreading the gospel the centerpiece of our marriage.

To realize that mission, I spent many hours a day working on the church, sometimes from 8 a.m. to midnight. Cheryl stayed at home with the kids, but before she was sick, she was involved at the church in all the ways her schedule allowed, leading our Vacation Bible School in the summertime, doing administrative tasks up at the offices of the church every Friday, and deploying her humor and wit to deliver the announcements at each church service.

In a nutshell, the church was our life. We rarely took vacations, but when we did, we would go to a conference for church leaders and call it "vacation." Of course, it was not a break or a time to relax, rejuvenate, or get in quality time. Often the sessions would stretch from early morning until late into the evening, and the kids would spend all day with the other pastors' kids doing preplanned activities, barely seeing us at all. It was exhausting, it was work, but we didn't admit it. Instead, we saw it as a compromise we had to make, one that was furthering the mission, one that we had the vigor and energy to see through, one that we didn't realize was going to cost so much.

From 1986 on, as each year passed we added more ministries—counseling and Bible classes each evening, developing ministries for children and middle schoolers and high schoolers. Because of our growth, we went through eight different building projects, the biggest of which was the multimillion dollar church on forty acres that we completed in 2001, though that was shortly followed by another expansion because there simply weren't enough facilities for everything we were doing. Unsurprisingly, neither of us had any hobbies to speak of, nor friends we saw outside of church activities. Unsurprisingly, the church was also all we had to talk about.

It's possible that if Cheryl hadn't gotten sick, we could have kept working as partners in a mission. There might not have been intimacy, and we might not have felt very much affection toward one another, but things might have been sustainable. But Cheryl did fall ill. As her health deteriorated, she could do less and less, and as the stone gained speed as it rolled down the hill, I felt like I had no other choice but to carry on with the mission without her.

A well-known psychiatrist in Grand Junction was the one who explained how this mission phenomenon affects many couples in ministry. During his training at Wheaton College in Illinois, one of his clinical jobs was to counsel couples coming home from the mission field. Time after time, he saw the same thing taking place: young couples got involved in spreading the gospel, and without intending to, they made that the emphasis in the marriage instead of a commitment to one another, to meeting one another's needs. What resulted were dysfunctional marriages plagued by adultery and drug abuse, marriages that were teetering on the brink of divorce, especially when one half of the couple was no longer willing or able to go on with the mission.

We were not unlike those young kids. When we married, we had a youthful love, but did not allow it to mature into true intimacy and mutual respect. We believed that because we were working to build up the kingdom of God, he would take care of our marriage. But like them, we were teetering on the brink of divorce after neglecting one another for so long.

In hindsight, I know things could have been different. There are so many variables that if they had been a little bit differently arranged, we might have made it. If we had recognized that the marriage was more important than the mission, than the career, than the income. If we had recognized that we had to be a couple and not just a family. If we had realized that we really had to work to keep it together, that we couldn't let life distract us from the core of our relationship.

But we didn't do that, and by the time we knew things were bad, it was like a patient going to a doctor with stage-four cancer. For almost a decade after our children left the house, we did what we needed to do to get by and maintain the status quo. Because of our standing in our church and community, we maintained a façade that our marriage was good and healthy for years, but toward the end, the energy it took to keep up the pretense was just exhausting.

To try and fix things at that point—well, there was so much to battle that it was too late. Climbing that mountain was impossible. Cheryl felt the same way; even though I initiated the divorce, she actually saw a lawyer before I did.

I don't know that anybody who has been married will disagree that marriage is difficult. It's probably one of the most difficult relationships we'll ever be in, and in the last fifty years, the institution of marriage has been the most unstable that it has ever been.

Often in the church, we blame that instability on the country's failing moral compass or to some secular social movement. But if that were accurate, pollster George Barna's 1999 survey about marriage and divorce would not show born-again Christians to have the highest divorce rates of any group of adults in the United States, and his 2008 survey would not reflect that Christians of all stripes get divorced at almost identical rates as atheists and agnostics. These numbers undermine that idea that divorce is for people who don't regard marriage as a sacred covenant designed and implemented by the triune God.

These numbers also undermine the idea that marriage can be sustained if you just ask for God's help. For most of my married life, I truly believed that God would sustain my marriage—if I just trusted in him, if I prayed and fasted and relied on him enough, if I expelled the demons in our midst and asked for his hand to guide us. Yet my marriage still failed. My marriage did not keep going just because we got married in a church, because we loved the Lord and followed the rules of the church, or because I was doing "God's work."

And honestly, believing God was going to sustain my marriage actually led me to a place where I didn't take care of business. If I hadn't believed that God was responsible for our marriage, I might have taken responsibility for myself, and Cheryl might have done the same. If we had put our relationship at the center of our marriage instead of putting the mission at the center of our marriage, we might have had a stronger foundation. And if we had known that the idealized 1950s version of marriage that was so pervasive when we came of age was an inherently unstable institution, maybe we would have worked harder to give it some support.

But we didn't realize that marriage was inherently unstable. And despite the fact that the divorce rate was already climbing by the end of the 1950s, the long decade of *Ozzie and Harriet*-style marriages, many people still go into marriage thinking that forever is attainable for any couple who love each other enough. Despite the fact that the divorce rate hovers around 50 percent, every couple thinks they won't be the ones to divorce. But the odds are a toss-up, no matter if you are religious or not.

In her illuminating book *Marriage, A History,* Stephanie Coontz explains why this is the case. She argues that for many years, marriage was a far more stable—though much less equitable and overall less satisfying—institution than it is today. This was because romantic love and personal satisfaction were not the goal of the marriage. For both the upper and lower echelons of society, from the time of the ancient Hebrews through the time of the Roman Empire and on through the Middles Ages, marriage was an institution that served much more than the individual's need for romantic love. For the ruling class, it was a way to shore up political power as well as to keep wealth concentrated in a few hands. For the lower classes, life was hard work from sunup to sundown, and marriage was a way to split up the work, to have children to help with labor on the farm—in short, to ensure survival.

"Until the late eighteenth century, most societies around the world saw marriage as far too vital an economic and political institution to be left entirely to the free choice of the two individuals involved," Coontz writes early on in her book, "especially if they were going to base their decision on something as unreasoning and transitory as love."[4] To ensure their children made suitable matches, parents, grandparents, and even extended kin would weigh in on a match, either directly through an arranged marriage, or indirectly, by exerting pressure for or against a potential mate.

And what constituted a marriage has changed over time as well. To quote the King James version of the Bible, a marriage occurred when "he took her into his tent and knew her." It wasn't about having a church ceremony and having the union blessed by a preacher; it was far more practical than that. For the first millennium after Christ, marriage wasn't even a part of the church, nor was divorce. Those were family matters, and people married and dissolved marriages based on their individual needs.

In the Western world, marrying for love emerged as an ideal in the late 1800s, when ideas about human and individual rights were first surfacing, but it wasn't realized until my parents' generation. Many forces had prohibited marrying for love, but the main ones were economic forces: marrying for love didn't assure you that you would have food to eat. But in the 1950s, America and many other Western countries were experiencing the postwar economic boom, and with rising wages and greater employment opportunities, young people finally had the freedom and ability to marry who they wanted when they wanted, and to fashion the lives they wanted.

Almost universally, the changes that occurred in the structure and practice of marriage between the early nineteenth and late twentieth centuries were extremely good for individuals and for human rights, especially for women, who were no longer defined as the legal property of their husbands, and children, who were no longer treated as sources of labor. But what they weren't good for was the *stability* of marriage. In that arrangement, the nuclear family took on many responsibilities—emotional, psychological, symbolic, and social responsibilities—that had previously been spread out across networks of family and friends. At the same time that marriage was acquiring new responsibilities, it had fewer supports keeping it intact. You didn't have to stay married to keep the farm running. You didn't face a war between families or clans if you split up.

So when romantic love—that notoriously fickle, changeable emotion—turned sour, it was much easier to head for the door.

I am not saying this to attack the current institution of marriage or to advocate against it. I see couples in my work with hospice who have been married for decades and who are devastated that one will have to go on without the other. In the wake of my traumatic divorce, these people are hope for me.

But I do think it's important that we recognize the facts without judgment: that Christians and non-Christians are vulnerable to failed marriages. That marriage has changed over time, given the political, economic, and social climates of the world. That marriage based on romantic love is an inherently unstable institution that requires endless patience, endless compromise, and lots of love and forgiveness and understanding. That there is no ideal marriage, and that the past wasn't filled with perfect marriages.

Divorce is not something that one should reach for at the drop of a hat. It's an intensely personal, intensely difficult, intensely painful decision. I don't know of anything that destroys relationships like divorce, not only within the immediate family, but also in extended family and with friends and acquaintances.

But without reserve, I believe divorce is a necessary thing. I know that Jesus forbids divorce in the New Testament, but I also know that God granted divorce to Moses because imperfect human beings got coupled in relationships that didn't work out. If we look at contemporary statistics, divorce plays an incredibly important role. As Coontz explains in *Marriage, a History,* "[U]nilateral divorce provides an important escape mechanism in seriously troubled marriages. Economists Betsey Stevenson and Justin Wolfers found that in states that adopted unilateral divorce, this was followed, on average, by a 20 percent reduction in the number of married women committing suicide, as well as a significant drop in domestic violence for both men and women," as well as fewer homicides against women. Even more stunning are the statistics on how divorce reduces the number of men who are victims in a bad marriage. "The Centers on Disease Control reports that the rate at which husbands were killed by their wives fell by approximately two-thirds between 1981 and 1998," Coontz writes, "in part because women could more easily leave their partners."[5]

To me, this seems like common sense. Several years ago, I watched part of the murder trial of Scott Peterson, accused of murdering his wife, Stacy, who was pregnant with their first child. I can remember watching Stacy's mother taking the stand and saying simply, "Divorce. Not murder. Divorce." I heard that and I thought, *She's right. That's the key.* For some people, divorce is the only outlet, and it has to be there.

These examples are extreme, I know, but medical evidence shows that troubled marriages that don't lead to something as dire as suicide or murder can still have a negative impact. Coontz notes that marriage does have health benefits for some. "But individuals in unhappy marriages are *more* psychologically distressed than people who stay single, and many of marriage's health benefits fade if the marriage is troubled," Coontz writes. "A three-year study of married couples in which the partner had mild hypertension found that...for those who were unhappily married, a few extra minutes of time together raised the blood pressure of the at-risk spouse. Having an argumentative or highly critical spouse can seriously damage a person's health, raising blood pressure, lowering immune function, and even worsening the symptoms of chronic illnesses like arthritis."[6]

By the end of our marriage, Cheryl and I had run the gamut. We were married for thirty-seven years, and by that time, I had contemplated suicide and we had both wished for the other's death as a way out. My mental and physical well-being was extremely compromised, and who knows what effect the constant stress of our failing marriage had on Cheryl's already poor health?

Had we just been honest with one another and less afraid of the stigma of divorce, we might have saved ourselves and many people around us a great deal of pain.

By the time I had my breakdown, I felt like I had settled into my life—as father, as husband, as pastor—so permanently, so irrevocably, that this unhappy marriage was my lot. It was hard to imagine that it could be different. We had been going through counseling and to therapists. We went on a weeklong marriage retreat. Nothing was working.

This is something I see all the time in Christians: they are waiting on God to make a tough decision for them, and they can't make it themselves.

A year after my breakdown, I retired and was in the house with Cheryl most of the day for several months, and our interactions were either nonexistent or almost unbearable. During that time, Canyon View paid for us to attend a second weeklong retreat. But it was too late. A few days in, one counselor who had been working with us looked at me with so much understanding in her eyes, and she said, "Not all marriages make it."

We were one of those.

Within a few months, I was at a place where I didn't care anymore. Some small argument sent me over the edge, and I just said, "That's it." The fear of what would happen if I stayed was far greater than what I faced if I left. I packed up my clothes and moved out. Soon after, our son, Jon, moved in with Cheryl and lived with her until she died three years later.

By the time I left, I had been through so much pain that leaving was just a relief. I can look back on that moment in the courtroom the day Cheryl and I were getting a divorce, and I know it was the right thing to do. I knew it on that day too. There was a piece of me that knew that what I was doing, I had to do. That was my walk.

What I do regret is that I hurt others, particularly my children. I saw they had been hurt because we made our mission the foundation of our marriage and failed to nurture our relationship before it was too late; hurt because of our contentment with the status quo and our belief that God would sustain our marriage; hurt because we refused to address our problems in an honest, loving, respectful way.

More than anything, I saw that they were hurt by my desperation at the end—by my hypocrisy and my infidelity, by my actions that were a direct contradiction to the man I said I was. Because of this, they were placed in an impossible situation, forced to endure my humiliating fall from grace from the pedestal I had climbed up on as a pastor. So with all of my heart, I regret the pain I have caused them and the damage I have done to my relationships with them.

But as I explained to our oldest daughter when we split up, our marriage had died long before any divorce made it official. Our hearts had hardened to one another, and I finally understood what Jesus was saying when he warned against hardness of the heart, because I couldn't muster compassion or understanding or any shred of love anymore. Anything that had ever been sacred was gone. Staying together was no longer an option.

And even if it had been, it would only have been out a sense of obligation mixed with fear. Fear of God's judgment, obligation to our vows. Recently I spoke to a couple who explained to me that they were staying together because of their vows. They can't stand one another. She hates him and wishes he'd have an affair so she would have an excuse to leave, and he wishes that she would die, but they stay because of their vows. They are miserable, and they are harboring this disdain for one another, and I just want to throw up my hands and ask, "So, God's really impressed that you stay together because of the vows even though you hate one another?" And then I want to shout the old verse from first Samuel—*Man looks on the outward appearance, but God looks on the heart! How you are in your heart matters!*

I look back on my days as a pastor, and I wish I had understood that. I wish I had counseled people to stop forcing themselves into something that was killing them. I wish I had been able to see the areas in the Bible where marriage did not match our contemporary narrative, where Moses abandoned his wife in the middle of the desert, where Peter left his wife to follow Christ, where Paul might have done the same. I wish that I had seen that these were all people doing God's work, but whose marriages failed miserably.

Yet I didn't, and it's because we can't allow space for divorce. Think about it: how many times have you heard a sermon about Zipporah? How God was going to kill Moses because his son wasn't circumcised, so she had their son circumcised, threw the foreskin at his feet, and said, "You are a man of death to me." We never hear from her again.

But I didn't have those exceptions in mind when people came for counsel, not even when a close personal friend came to me and said, "I can't do it anymore." Instead of offering compassion and believing that he might know his life better than I did, I exhorted him to stick with it. "You gotta do this!" I said to him. "This is God's way!"

He had shared all the reasons he needed out, all the reasons he was just breaking under the pressure, and yet I was putting the thumb on him to stay in it no matter what. In the end, I was just like the Pharisees Jesus condemned when he said, "You people, you put loads and weights on people that you are not willing to bear." After my own failed marriage, I could only apologize to my friend and ask forgiveness for my stubbornness and arrogance.

I realize that it sounds convenient for me to advocate for divorce now, that I sound like I am trying to excuse my own behavior. But I am not interested in repairing how I appear to the world. Instead, this is me realizing the old adage about walking a mile in someone else's shoes—unless you've done it, you probably shouldn't judge.

And I can admit now that I judged wrongly. I can admit that I was not understanding. I can admit that I was a hypocrite.

Because when I pressured my friend to stay in his marriage, I was trying to speak to something that I had no idea about. Without taking into account the difficulty he was living with, I advised him as if one answer was applicable to every situation. But one-size-fits-all doesn't work; it's a simplified response to a complex situation.

It is true that we have social institutions that bring stability, and that's a good thing. I believe marriage is one of those good, stable social institutions. A stable, healthy marriage as an institution has tremendous benefits to the individuals involved, and it occupies an important place in our collective consciousness. I also very much believe that a stable, healthy marriage and family is the best place to raise children.

Given its benefits, and knowing the costs of divorce, I think that most people who marry try their hardest to stay together. But sometimes, people just can't work it out, and past a certain point, staying in the marriage has negative consequences that far outweigh the benefits. At a certain point, the mental and emotional health of both the children and the parents are compromised. At a certain point, the parents will be modeling poor relationships, which will become the child's frame of reference in the future. Instead of insisting that people stay together no matter what the cost, the church needs to be more flexible, to allow this space for our human imperfections and marital stalemates, to offer grace.

And instead of blaming outside causes for divorce, the church needs to take a look at itself and see where it can do a better job of supporting the institution of marriage. As George Barna astutely pointed out in his 1999 report, "[T]he high incidence of divorce within the Christian community challenges the idea that churches provide truly practical and life-changing support for marriages." The church needs to do a better job of communicating the realities of marriage, counseling those considering marriage, and offering services to those who are struggling in their marriages.

And when people have run the gamut of options—prayer and counseling and practical solutions for their marriage conflicts—and they are still in a miserable, hopeless, loveless marriage, the church needs to find a way to accept their decision to divorce and offer support to them afterward. I can admit now that when I was a pastor, I was wrong in refusing to do so. I believed a couple who divorced were just giving up. I believed they were taking the easy way out—as if dissolving the most intimate and important relationship in one's life is the easy way out!

Sadly, Christians know when they are being ostracized because of their failed marriages. In the wake of his 1999 report about divorce, George Barna explained that for Christians who experience a divorce, "Many of them feel their community of faith provides rejection rather than support and healing," and quite rightly, he sees this as more condemnable than the divorce itself. Again, the place that is supposed to provide compassion, love, and healing turns into the sharp tool of judgment.

I think that judgment is misplaced, like so much of our human judgment. I have waded through this quandary for several years, and I have asked myself real, searching questions that my disillusionment has allowed.

Like: Are we as Christians supposed to stay in a marriage that destroys our minds and bodies? Are we supposed to stick with it even if we are so miserable that we wish for one or the other to die so that we can escape it? Is God more interested in preserving the institution than he is in saving the individual?

It took many years for me to get here, but I believe that God is more interested in saving the individual, that he is merciful, that he knows we are on a spiritual pilgrimage, on a long faith journey.

It took me many years to believe that when the marriage fails, his grace is there, and what he expects from us is to offer the same.

CHAPTER 8

BUILDING AN ILLUSION

These days, I find myself in a strange space, where I simply don't know the answers to various theological questions that I used to have no doubts about. Five years ago, I wouldn't have been able to admit this. But today, I'm surprisingly comfortable here. I'm comfortable saying, "I just don't know."

I'm comfortable saying, "I have so much hope, but I'm not sure of the answer to that."

That's not to say that I'm not searching, but since my disillusionment, I have been stripped of all my certainties, as well as the arrogance that went with them.

In my job as chaplain at a hospice center, I counsel and try to give comfort, context, and support to those who are terminally ill, as well as their families. It's very different from my role as pastor, though I still face some of the same challenges, where people hear the title "chaplain" and think of a minister, then put up a wall or make an excuse about why they don't go to church very often. That they think I am going to judge them really breaks my heart. They are struggling enough without that, so I try to dispel their anxieties by just being with them.

If I can cross that invisible boundary that the word "chaplain" conjures, often the patients and their families begin trusting me with their questions and their confidences. They might ask me about heaven or salvation or if I think God will heal their loved one. Many times, I have to say that I don't know, but that I am here with them, to hope with them, to listen with an open ear and without judgment, to offer empathy and love.

As the pastor of Canyon View Vineyard, I didn't offer any of that. I saw everything in black and white then, and I never said, "I don't know."

Instead, I gave them platitudes. I might fall back on Romans 8, verse 28: "All things work together for good for those who love God and are called according to his purpose."

Looking back at the number of times I used that just kills me. When people were going through a hard time, I pulled out a Bible verse and applied it to everything. Romans 8:28 was broad enough to work for good or bad, so it was an easy go-to, but I am ashamed of how unfeeling I was. I might be sitting in my office with a couple who had lost a child, and I would fall back on Romans 8:28. The parents would look at me like I had just fallen off Mars, and rightfully so. How does that one verse fill the gaping hole where their beloved child used to be? How could I expect them in that moment to think that their grief could ever be for good? At a moment of extreme, earth-shattering loss, I give them that verse, and they are left thinking, *How could a loving God intentionally take my child away and break my heart?* After seeing many people suffer the heartbreak that is part of our human condition, that logic doesn't make sense to me anymore. I can no longer spin tragedy as "God's perfect timing," as I used to do all the time.

Or I'd tell someone to "pray through"—pray through whatever trial you have and you will get the answer you want. If you pray through, circumstances will change in your life and things will get better.

When they didn't get better, I could say it again.

Or tell them, "Give it to God."

Or, "Everything happens for a reason."

Or if they were struggling financially, I'd tell them to make sure they were tithing, and God would pour out material blessings in abundance. When they would return months later with the same woes, I would sit behind my desk feeling like a defense attorney for a bad client. I had promised them that God would come through and ease their struggles, and that hadn't happened. Scripture said one thing, but experience was something else. Because I didn't have anything else to say, I'd counter with another platitude: "Well, we just don't understand the ways of God."

When this happened, I could see a person's faith crumbling. They'd soon leave the church, thinking, *You sold me a bill of goods.* Somewhere deep down, I worried that I had.

But did I admit that tension, even to myself?

No, I didn't. I couldn't.

Instead, it would all happen in God's perfect timing, and they should just pray through and remember that all things work together for good. There were no other possibilities in our worldview.

In the church, we try to sell certainties.

We make our religion into a bulwark against life's difficulties, as if there is a formula that will force God to move in our lives and protect us from hardship or suffering. As if our behavior will win us God's favor. As if our faith, if strong enough, will literally cast mountains into the sea. As if God will suspend natural law each time we ask, because we tell ourselves we have earned it. As if saying "I don't know," or thinking that there might be another way, would put us on the outs with God.

For many years, I pushed myself to believe it all beyond a shadow of a doubt. I attended church, tithed, worshiped, prayed, served, and even made sure to do right by my civic duties, like voting. Every morning, I had quiet times, where I would read and study the Bible, write in a journal, and pray and meditate. In my mind, these things all had a purpose. I thought all of those activities were molding me into a mature Christian, and I did these things and taught them as a way to connect with God, to be part of his people set apart.

One Sunday toward the end of my time at Canyon View Vineyard, I was delivering a sermon to that huge congregation. At the time, my personal life was in the absolute disarray I have described: my wife was terribly ill, my marriage was broken, my children were distant, and it had taken everything in me just to write the Sunday sermon. As I stood up at the front waxing eloquent about faith and God's perfect timing and the power of prayer, I just thought, *How can you be preaching this while your life is falling apart?*

It was a wake-up call, where I realized that I didn't have it figured out, that after so many years of absolute belief, the formula had failed. To my horror, those platitudes I had lived and taught for so long suddenly seemed hollow. The words that were coming out of my mouth were so far from my lived experience that the whole thing seemed absurd.

Part of my disillusionment was realizing that I had built an entire framework of beliefs and lived by a set of behaviors that were supposed to be my refuge, my buffer from the storm, but somehow, the wind and rain were upon me. I couldn't find God anywhere, and after looking to the platitudes for so long as certainties, as safeguards, as near-tangible realities, I had no idea where I'd find shelter.

As I said before, these days I am more comfortable not knowing.

I am comfortable using a more lenient code of ethics to guide my actions. I've come to believe that a lot of our rules and prohibitions are born out of our finite human minds.

Which is to say, I am no longer certain that God is offended by the same things we are.

And I may offer up a prayer, but I'm no longer convinced that God will hear it or answer it in a way that I understand. I am comfortable with the fact that I'll say a prayer one day, and that day will be good, then say the same prayer the next day, and it will be the worst day of the whole month.

I am comfortable saying, "Inscrutable your ways, O Lord," and moving on.

But why did it take me so long to get here?

There are a few things I could probably point to, all of which I have come to believe are of human invention, not divine. In the course of its two-thousand-year history, the Christian faith has developed a lot of doctrines about belief and behavior, and often, they are incredibly clear-cut. There are some things that are considered negotiable, like whether or not to baptize infants. But for the most part, Christian orthodoxy has been established, and as time has passed, those views have become more and more entrenched. On many issues, like the right to life or sex outside of marriage or salvation, there are no gray areas. Instead, the church has drawn on both biblical injunctions and traditional practices to sketch the world in two colors and allow very little room for gray.

But I think it us our humanness that causes us to do this. I think we do this because it makes us feel like things are simple and that we are safe.

Those who adhere to fundamentalist readings of the Bible, or even those who aren't fundamentalist but have their interpretation predetermined by their denomination, would disagree with me. They would say that things *are* black and white and would find passages of Scripture they can point to and say, "This is what God says; therefore, my worldview is correct. There is no other way." I can understand that way of thinking; I used to be in that camp.

Yet my lived experience has so often contradicted those answers that I have reached the point that I cannot see things that simply anymore. I have realized the gray areas comprise much of our lives.

Now that my paradigm has shifted and I do not have to see the Bible through a predetermined lens, I find many contradictions in Scripture, and I find many passages that can be read several different ways. I can admit that theologians of every stripe have argued doctrinal themes like faith versus works, the end of days, free will, the nature of the Trinity, and the features of heaven and hell until they are blue in the face, but none have ever proven their case beyond a shadow of a doubt, which is why Christendom is filled with so many denominations professing both stark and subtle differences in doctrine. For some questions, like the nature of God, I can read through Scripture myself and see descriptions of the vengeful, wrathful God who inflicts suffering and of the merciful God who is the source of all that is loving and good. I see places where God was close by and ever-present, and then I see the hundreds of years of silence, when he did not speak to his people.

What am I to make of these contrasts?

I used to think that I had to be certain about every little detail, and that I had to come down on one side or the other.

But recently I reached the point where I concluded that the ambiguity of it all—the uncertainty, the gray, the holding opposites in tension—is the definition of faith. Faith is not certainty, but the opposite. Faith is believing despite the fact that we can't prove it. Faith is believing without needing to put our hand in Jesus' side.

From where I stand now, I think I needed certainties before because that was what people told me faith was: not having any doubts or questions. I think that I, like many others, feared the unknown; and I, like many others, had trouble keeping these paradoxes straight in my head.

Modern believers are not alone in this struggle. For an ancient example, we only have to look again to the story of John the Baptist—this time to his father Zechariah, who finds himself in a situation where he needs some certainty in his walk with God. We learn in the Gospel of Luke that, though they have lived a blameless and righteous life, Zechariah and his wife Elizabeth are unable to conceive; but one day, as he is burning an offering of incense in the temple of the Lord, the archangel Gabriel appears to Zechariah and says, "Your wife is going to conceive and you will have a son."

But to Zechariah, this announcement makes no sense. Their reality is pretty black and white: he and his wife are old, and they have always been barren. So Zechariah asks the archangel for proof or certainty: "How shall I know this?"

Because Zechariah cannot simply accept the paradox but instead asks for proof, Gabriel strikes him mute until John is born.

The thing is, I think Zechariah's response is understandable. I think my response would have been similar: *This is crazy! How could this possibly come to pass?*

Truthfully, I have always been more of a Zechariah type, looking for proof and really wanting to know things objectively. But in the past five years, I don't have answers for what has happened in my life, and I've been able to draw comfort from the parallel story in Luke: when Gabriel appears to Mary and says she will bear a son, and his name shall be *Emmanuel,* which means "God with us."

Unlike Zechariah, Mary doesn't ask questions. She simply says, "Be it done." Interestingly, she has to be just as confused, and maybe even more so, since she has not been with a man. But she accepts the paradox. She accepts the contradiction. She doesn't ask for proof or for an answer. She simply says, "I will live in this tension. I am not sure how in the world this is going to work, but be it done unto me." I see Mary's response as a true and pure example of faith, one we should emulate.

Too often we are more like Zechariah, needing proof, needing a hard and fast answer. Too often we search for and create certainties that are more human than divine.

And that has a real impact on people.

When we create our certainties, we work to solidify the *form* of our faith, though not necessarily the heart of it. We build a framework that gives an illusion of reality, a faith that we feel is concrete, like the walls of our houses or the floors beneath our feet. We come up with rules and rituals that show we are abiding in that faith.

When we do that, we convince ourselves that we are taken care of, saved, "in." Life can be confusing when we're not certain of the outcome, so we fall back on Romans 8:28 and our rules and rituals to reassure ourselves that we'll be okay.

But I think we really need to stop and ask ourselves: Is this what Jesus was all about?

What does it mean to be a true follower of Christ, a true seeker of God?

Does it mean we go to church on Sunday? Does it mean we believe Romans 8:28, and we never doubt? Does it mean we follow all the rules? Does it mean that we live inside a prescribed lifestyle, performing the prescribed rituals our pastors have given us?

And what is the point of following Christ? To get into heaven? To make sure we are on God's good side, so he can help us out when we need it?

For a long time, I would have answered "yes" to those questions.

But lately, I have been asking a different set, though I'm not sure of the answers.

Lately I have been asking myself, Are those things just a form? Are these easy patterns to follow that make us feel like we are protected from life's storms, that we are set apart in God's eyes? Is it all a way we make ourselves feel better than those who are not like us?

These questions are not new. They've been debated again and again, in many different faith traditions over many hundreds of years, especially with regard to rules and rituals. In the time of Jesus, the Torah controlled every aspect of a Jewish person's life, both private and public. According to Geza Vermes, a scholar of ancient Judaism, the law dictated what crops you grew, how you did business, what you ate and how you prepared it, your sex life, and even your dress. From the Ten Commandments Moses received on Mount Sinai, along with further instructions in Exodus, Leviticus, Numbers, and Deuteronomy, the Jewish people developed 613 positive and negative commandments that all observant Jews should follow, and Orthodox Jews today still live by many of these.

And though Christianity began by eschewing much of the law of Moses, we soon developed our own set of rules and rituals. The liturgical side of the church has obvious ones. During Catholic masses, there are times to kneel, sit, or stand; there are prayers and responses to be memorized. There are also rules about eating meat during Lent, and in the more traditional parts of the church, women wear lace veils over their heads during Mass as a way of showing reverence for God.

Sometimes Protestants think they are free from such things. But in my own upbringing, certain doctrines were nonnegotiable, and conversion was not so much to Christ as it was to a lifestyle, where you agreed to speak and act and even dress like the rest of the congregation. Although there weren't formal rituals, there were definitely ways we behaved and performed to exhibit our faith. One was speaking in tongues. Sometimes this did happen authentically, but there was also enough pressure that someone might feel compelled to pretend in order to fit in with the group. Another ritual, which is performed more widely in many Protestant faiths, is the altar call. When our pastor stood at the front delivering emotional and fervent calls for repentance and pleadings for people to commit (or recommit) their lives to Christ, people fell in line and walked down to the front to prove that they were saved, that they were in.

The way I see it, each version of the Christian religion develops its own trappings, even if it begins as an individual founding a totally new movement in an attempt to leave behind the established denominations. That person may have a conviction, and soon enough, the leader has transferred his convictions onto his congregation. It might be a certain Bible verse that is the default, like Jeremiah 29:11: "For I know the plans I have for you, says the Lord, plans to prosper you, not to harm you!" Maybe it's about abstaining from alcohol, or how to participate in worship. Soon the patterns develop, and the new movement suddenly has a recognizable framework. It gets to the point where there are even predictable speech patterns. You can find them in the Mormon community, in the Pentecostal community, and in the Baptist community. Sometimes it's a physical movement, like at a nondenominational church here in Grand Junction where I've seen the ladies all nod their heads when the pastor is speaking. You look down the row and see four or five ladies nodding their heads. Why? It seems to me that there is nothing inherently holy about nodding heads. It seems more like it's the thing to do.

So it raises the question: Why do we follow these rules and rituals?

Is it because we feel them to be the only and authentic way to connect with God?

Is it because we think they get us into heaven?

Is it because that's what our parents taught us to do?

Is it because we are afraid of what others will think if we don't?

Is it because we are afraid that God will cast us out of his favor if we don't play along?

Of course, the answer to these questions varies from person to person.

For some, following the rules and rituals truly makes them feel connected to God.

For others, it is a form that has no heart, no content. It is something they participate in out of habit. They go through the motions without feeling a thing. It is something they do because they worry what others will think—that if they stay in their seats during the altar call, or if they don't baptize their child in infancy, or if they don't keep kosher, their neighbors will judge them. Maybe they repeat the Bible verse because they don't know what else to say, and if they were to admit that they struggled with Romans 8:28, they'd be ostracized. Maybe some people follow the form even if they don't believe in it because they are afraid about what will happen if they don't. *What if it is true?* they ask themselves. *What will God do to me if I refuse?*

I want to be very clear when I say that the form is not the issue here. I think different people feel connected to God in very different ways, and I believe that's right and good. We are unique people. We are at different places, with varied experiences and different spiritual and emotional lives. It makes sense to me that we would reach for different forms in order to connect with God.

But if we would look closely and honestly, we'd see that often, as we add and add and add doctrines and rules and rituals, there is more and more of an opportunity to get caught up in the form. When this happens, believers can begin to substitute the form for the content. As Meister Eckart, the medieval Christian mystic, said, "If you focus too narrowly on a single path to God, all you will ever find is the path."

Which is another way of saying that we begin substituting the form of religion for a true and dynamic connection with God, and substituting following the rules for following Christ.

You may ask, So what? What does it matter?

The problem I see is that when we are focused on the form instead of true connection with God, our eyes are on the external but not the internal. And it is my belief that worrying about the external diverts us from our true mission as followers of Christ, which is a call to offer the unconditional love of God the Father and Jesus his Son to a broken and suffering world.

Instead, we look with critical eyes to make sure that everyone is on the "right" path.

This, of course, happens in varying degrees, with the most legalistic denominations being the worst offenders. Take the example of my childhood. When I was growing up, women were basically to stay at home, take care of the family, make sure that the house was clean, and be sure the kids were well-trained and behaving. Men were to provide the material needs for the family as well as the spiritual guidance. Our belief was that people only went awry under the influence of evil. If your life was in order and your family was in shape, it was proof of God's favor, which is another version of the prosperity gospel.

Though it was the most intense in my childhood church, this type of thinking was prevalent in almost every church I've been a part of since then, and it seems like the more black and white the doctrine, and the more certain people are of their own religion's righteousness, the more likely they are to issue these types of judgments.

I have seen the judgment happen in the church so much that it pains me. When I was growing up, if a girl got pregnant she was totally ostracized. There was no love, no acceptance for who she was, no compassion for what she was going through. The parents were judged and blamed too—they obviously weren't doing a good job. So the institution that was supposed to be a place of love, compassion, and healing suddenly became the sharp instrument of judgment. Given the message of Christ, that judgment is a contradiction in every way, shape, and form.

I do not say this to condemn others without any self-awareness. I know that I am not above reproach in this arena; it causes me sorrow that I was both a participant in and a recipient of judgment. But I'm not sure how we got to this place or why we are holding on to such attitudes, given the fact that both the Old and the New Testaments warn against judgment. In the first book of Samuel, the Lord says, "Man looks at the outward appearance, but the Lord looks at the heart." The Lord is saying that we are clueless about his judgment, and that we don't even look in the right places! In several places in the Gospels, Jesus tells us not to judge. He draws a line in the sand and says that only the blameless should throw stones. He points out that we ignore our own glaring faults but feel comfortable calling out our brothers. He tells us not to judge because our judgment is flawed; as finite human beings, we cannot know the whole story.

Yet even with all these lessons against judging, we are still so quick to pass judgment!

That judgment has repercussions within our Christian communities. It stunts our ability to develop our God-given discernment; it prevents us from abiding by our own consciences. I realize now that instead of developing my own personal convictions, I allowed the judgment of people in my faith community to monopolize the way I lived my life. How often did I stand at the crossroads of a decision and, instead of being motivated by my own internal compass, was I motivated to capitulate to what the other people in the church would say or how they would react?

Too many times to count.

In my many years of ministry, I've seen countless individuals whose first worry isn't what is best for them but what others in the church will think. If they are caught having a glass of wine, what will others think? Even now, if their daughter gets pregnant, they are afraid of what others will think. If their son quits attending church, what will others think? In this system, the two most important figures—the individual and their God—are summarily ignored.

It is surprising to realize how much suffering people will endure because of fear that their fellow believers will judge them. Most people in the church who have a bad marriage will never speak about it anywhere within the church. It's the same in any area that the church deems taboo. Sometimes people disregard the church's rules because they don't feel personally convicted, and they simply hide their "deviance." They aren't honest about it because they know they'd be preached at.

Our judgment turns people into sneaks.

As I've explained before, I have come to think that one of the biggest sins within the church is pretense. We make ourselves look alike, and we pretend to feel and think alike, and we are even pressured to vote alike. Things are all decided for us, and we are supposed to fall in line. But the model we strive to emulate—Jesus Christ—wasn't that way. He broke the mold. He stressed mercy and forgiveness and unconditional love at a time and in a culture that was much more concerned with legalism. With that model in mind, I think it's high time for the church to take a step back and look at itself and ask, "What message are we really sending? Is it mercy? Is it forgiveness? Is it love? Do we prioritize loving people?"

And if our answer is no, that we do not prioritize loving people over the structures and strictures of the organization, then we need to reevaluate. We need to reexamine the model of Jesus and find a way to do what he did. We need to figure out a way to love people where they are, even if we don't agree with their lifestyles or with choices they have made.

Jesus had harsh words for those who worried about the external rather than the internal, who lived the form but had no heart of love. "Woe to you, teachers of the law and Pharisees, you hypocrites!" Jesus exclaims in Matthew 23. "You give a tenth of your spices—mint, dill and cumin. But you have neglected the more important matters of the law—justice, mercy and faithfulness. You should have practiced the latter, without neglecting the former."

"You blind guides!" he says. "You strain out a gnat but swallow a camel." You focus on the tiny infractions, Jesus is telling them (and us), but you neglect the bigger picture.

And the critique keeps coming. The Pharisees clean the outside of the cup and dish, but they neglect the inside, which is full of greed and self-indulgence. They are like whitewashed tombs: beautiful on the outside, but inside full of death, unclean. In the same way, on the outside they appear to be righteous, but on the inside, they are full of hypocrisy and wickedness.

Just because things look good on the outside doesn't mean our hearts are pure.

Just because we live the letter of the law doesn't mean we understand the spirit.

Just because we follow the rules and rituals does not mean our hearts are reaching for the Lord or working to bring about his kingdom.

In fact, in his forceful criticism of the Pharisees in Matthew 23, Jesus condemned the human tendency to focus on the external, of confusing the form for the content; instead, he emphasized the *ethical* over the *ritual*.[7] Again, as Geza Vermes points out, this was one of Jesus's main differences from his Jewish contemporaries—his emphasis on the internal value of following God's law rather than the external. He was concerned with a person's heart, with his or her pure intentions. In Matthew 5, Jesus says that being angry with your brother or sister will incur judgment alongside someone who has committed murder.

In the same way, your intention when you do follow commandments is what matters. "Charitable gifts must be made in secret, without witnesses," Vermes writes in a summary of Jesus's teachings to his followers. "Prayer is to be offered in private, not aloud in the streets or synagogue. Fasting is to be undertaken with a smiling face, before God alone."[8]

So the attitude, or the internal, was as important as the act, the external.

One of the most important reasons to follow this teaching of Jesus is because of some very practical implications. When we are focused on the integrity of our faith rather than on how someone else is going to look at us, we are focused on our own hearts. In my experience, when I am focused on my heart and not on how I look, I don't worry about how others look. I don't worry about the speck in my neighbor's eye instead of the plank in my own. Because I'm focused on my own heart, which is what God sees, I don't fall into the trap of letting my religion make me feel like I'm better than other parts of God's creation.

However, when we feel like we have it figured out and others don't—if we decide that a certain mode of worship or belief is better than another—we become convinced of our own superiority. We derive a sense of entitlement from or privilege with God because of our faith; we use it as a way to make us feel set apart.

It is interesting to note that the religious people of Jesus's day were individuals who practiced isolation from the society they inhabited, and who followed rules and regulations that determined whether they were in or out. The word Pharisee translates as "separated one," a testament to their belief that distance from others who were not like them was not only beneficial to their faith but was also godly. And with those six hundred laws and practices, it was easy to distinguish between those who remained in the group and those who had traded in their membership. "Everything they do is done for people to see," Jesus says in Matthew 23. "They make their phylacteries wide and the tassels on their garments long."

How much have Christians done this over the years? How much have we built up doctrines and rules and rituals that prove to one another that we are in?

How much time and effort do we exert in following rules and denying our doubts so that we can feel like we are safe, saved, and in?

How much time does that leave us for actually living out the radical message of Jesus, to love God and to love our neighbor?

For me, these were startling realizations. More than startling, it was devastating when I realized that the framework I had built was an illusion, that things weren't as black and white as I had always believed. In my arrogance, I thought I had God figured out, and that I could force his hand in my life because of what I believed and because I followed the rules. Yet it didn't work out that way. God can't be put in a neat little formula of faith, and when we try to—when we try to sell our faith as a certainty—we are setting people up for disillusionment, and for the absolute confusion and devastation that accompanies a broken dream.

After a lifetime of church membership, I am disillusioned with what we as humans have created. I am disillusioned with the church as an exclusive club for those who profess the right things and act the right way. I long for the day when the church is an inclusive organism, free of judgment, fluid and flexible enough to accept the gray areas and the paradoxes in life, where we are searching for a dynamic relationship with the Father.

And in my mind, we should approach this enterprise with humility and openness. As human beings, we are so limited, so finite. We have trouble understanding other humans—individuals with brains like ours and the same earthly experience and modes of communicating. Given these limits, it's astounding that we think we can figure God out and put him in a rigid framework or formula.

Because simply put, we will never completely comprehend God or his ways. Years ago, I heard Francis Schaeffer talk about the "absolute wonder of God." As humans, we can think about how there is a future, and we can imagine how there is no end, but to think that there was never a beginning is the absolute of wonders. That there was an uncaused first cause is impossible for humans to comprehend; to think that God has always been is just beyond us, and that demonstrates our finiteness. We cannot define God. In the course of human history, we have had little glimpses of who he is. To Moses, he was a burning bush. To Elijah, he was a still, small voice. Of course, when Jesus came, he revealed God in a new way; however, Jesus' revelation was not all of one kind either: To Paul, he was a blinding light, chastising and chastening. To the woman who washed his feet with her tears, he was gentle and gracious.

To even try to define the height or depth of God's grace is either the height of arrogance or the depths of stupidity, because we don't know. To stand around and say, "God is like this, not that" or "Because of that person's actions, he or she will be condemned to an eternity without God" is arrogant. Again, from Paul: "We all see through a glass darkly." That means everybody—everybody sees through a glass darkly. Nobody has it completely right.

I wish it hadn't taken me so long to figure that out. I wish that there had been more space in my belief system for abundance and fluidness and grace. I wish that, instead of getting hung up on the form and on judging people based on our strict criteria, I would have noted some truth in this Buddhist saying about our doctrines and rules and rituals: "Everything we do to understand God is the finger pointing at the moon, but it is not the moon."

I wish I had realized long ago that the lines we have created within the church as to who is in and who is out aren't as bold and clear as we would like to believe, and that sometimes there are no easy answers.

Now, I have shifted my focus. I hardly ever worry about getting into heaven. Instead, I try to focus on bringing about heaven here on earth. It seems to me that's what Jesus's mission was. I love the verse in the book of Acts that says Jesus went about doing good—he went about healing, he went about loving, he went about restoring things that were broken. There was plenty left to do when he ascended, and so that's our lot. I realize now that the best I can do is offer counsel and comfort to people who are suffering, to make them laugh when they need a laugh, or to let them cry when they need to cry. The best I can do is to tell them the truth: that there are no easy answers, but we do have reason to love.

Because as another verse in Romans 8 tells us, our greatest hope is God's love and mercy. In verse 38, Paul writes, "For I am convinced that neither death, nor life, nor angels, nor principalities, nor present things, nor future things, nor height, nor depth, nor any other creature will be able to separate us from the love of God in Christ Jesus our Lord."

To me, that means that God is bigger than we think, more merciful than we think, and more expansive and loving than any of our narrow doctrines will ever admit.

CHAPTER 9

CLEANING THE FISH

I t's surprising how completely the tables can turn.

When Cheryl and I returned to Grand Junction after our time in Afghanistan, we wanted to minister to the unchurched. In Grand Junction, there obviously wasn't the same intensity of countercultural activity that we had seen in Afghanistan, but there were young people asking the same types of questions. And one man, a guy named Rick Tomassi, radically converted to Christianity. Over a period of time, he shared his story about his conversion with his friends and acquaintances in this countercultural movement, and because of his enthusiasm and true heart, he gathered a following of about sixty young people. And they began attending our charismatic and fundamentalist church.

Our pastor wasn't sure what to do with them, and knowing that we had worked in countercultural circles in Afghanistan, he approached Cheryl and me and asked us to take them on. We happily agreed to lead a class for these new converts. We began helping these young seekers through the foundations of what it meant to be a Christian, which was phenomenal to watch. Yet these people really enjoyed the lifestyle they had been living. They loved the communal aspect of their lives. They enjoyed their folk music, staying up late at night, wearing long hair, and at the same time, talking about what God was doing in their lives. They didn't want to give that all up just because they had become Christians.

But here was where the two worlds collided.

As time went on, you could feel the church's need for control kicking in. Soon the pastor started getting notes and letters from older and more long-standing members of the congregation about how the kids were still smoking, about how they were breaking our rules of conduct. He came to us and asked what we were going to do about it.

We told him, "Pastor, these kids are asking big existential questions, and they are struggling and lonely and lost. They are seeking God and are desperately looking for a place where they are accepted. Smoking is the least of their problems."

But the church's rules were bigger than those kids, and it wasn't long before they'd all been driven away. It still almost brings me to tears, both for the young people who were truly searching for God, and for the church crowd, that they couldn't see what they were missing in refusing these young seekers. I can remember two of the young men who were incredibly talented musically, and they would write the most beautiful songs and play them during our services. When those two guys were up there, wearing their tie-dyed T-shirts and bell-bottoms with long hair and beads, singing songs about Jesus, there wasn't a dry eye in the place. Yet the church couldn't see the progress in these kids. The church needed them to change their lifestyle immediately. They needed them to be wearing a suit and tie and cutting out any behaviors that were against the norm. Once, someone described this to me as cleaning the fish before we catch them. It was a perfect example of how the policies and procedures of this organization were more important than the people they were trying to influence. I just wanted to say, "Please, just leave them alone. Just let them grow. Let them be who they are. God knows how to reach them and where they are. Just love them." It was incredibly frustrating.

But only a few years later, I was the pastor of Christian Life Center, which we held in an old Chrysler dealership. And I remember one man who came to our church and had a real conversion experience. He was so excited about following Christ and learning to read the Scriptures. One day he came in and told me about how he and a friend had gone out to a bar after work, and they'd had this wonderful conversation about God. And do you know what my gut reaction was?

You were at a bar.

I might not have said those words, but I certainly wasn't excited that he was sharing the message of Jesus and talking about the change in his life. Instead of rejoicing that he had found something that was going to propel him on in his spiritual journey, I was judging.

Somewhere down inside, I knew my reaction was wrong. But at the time, I saw that he wasn't following the rules of the club—that if he had truly converted, he would be doing it all our way. Now I realize that I was no different from the people who couldn't handle the hippies and their cigarettes.

How was it that I didn't see myself slipping into the same patterns of thought that had bothered me so much in others? The only thing I can figure out is that as time passed, and as I became the pastor and was expected to lead a certain type of life, I found myself conforming to the lifestyle of the church—the letter of the law—more and more.

I had lived in a space so full of judgment for so long that judgment was what I knew best.

I still have to fight the judgment sometimes, and it's not because I am adhering to the rules that once governed my whole life. Since I resigned as pastor of Canyon View Vineyard, my lifestyle has changed vastly. Besides a few years in high school and college, I abstained from alcohol and never stepped a foot into a bar; now I regularly hang out at a bar with my work friends after a day at the office. But for a long time, that residue of living a separated lifestyle still raised its ugly head when I headed into a bar or a casino. When I would go in and have a beer— because I finally could!—each time the door opened, I would swivel my head around to see who was walking in. The strange thing was, I was judging those who were coming in as much as I feared being judged for the same thing. And it took quite some time to get to the point where I could accept myself, where I could sit with my friends and really enjoy the environment, where I could settle in and say to myself, *This is what I was designed for. This is me without a pastor hat on. This is me.*

Now when people I know walk by and say, "Hello, Pastor," I say, "Just Dan." I feel free of so much bondage. When I am in a bar, I know I'm not sitting in a forbidden zone. I'm sitting in a place with friends, a place where my new faith is directing me, a place where I'm a part of the society I live in.

I'm not sure why it took me so long to realize that I wasn't evil for going to a bar, and it wasn't evil for others to do it either. I don't know why it took so long for me to realize that Jesus would have been there himself. A few years ago, I saw Franco Zeffirelli's film *Jesus of Nazareth,* which was released in 1977. After covering Jesus' birth and childhood, the film details his ministry as he moves around Galilee accompanied by his first disciples, Simon and his brother Andrew, as well as James and John, the sons of Zebedee. And as he travels along the sea, Jesus meets Matthew, a tax collector in Capernaum. As we know, tax collectors were widely reviled. They were considered traitors by their Jewish neighbors for their complicity with the Roman invaders in levying taxes, and doubly for their willingness to levy higher amounts for their own benefit. Matthew was one of those tax collectors who had grown wealthy on the backs of his own people by aligning himself with the Romans, and his people all knew it and hated him for it.

Yet Matthew was moved by Jesus. In the film, Matthew invites Jesus to dinner to learn who this charismatic teacher is. The disciples are unhappy that Jesus would make peace with this traitor or associate with Matthew's crowd. James says to him, "It is a scandal for you to eat with these people! We've lived our lives honorably, made sacrifices to keep the law. They are thieves, whores, usurers—violent and godless people. And now you sit and eat with such people, who spend their lives in orgies and perversions."

Undeterred, Jesus answers him, "I've not come to call the virtuous."

James tries again, telling Jesus he'll be contaminated, and the others agree.

"James," Jesus replies, "the heart of the Lord is mercy."

And Jesus attends this gathering at Matthew's home. In his robes the color of flax, Jesus steps into the courtyard where all the revelers wear dark reds, blues, blacks, and oranges. The camera cuts to people sitting on the ground, leaning drunkenly; to a voluptuous woman; then to a fight. There is wine flowing and belly dancers and raucous laughter that seems in line with a ribald joke. Jesus doesn't say anything or stop anyone. He doesn't condemn anyone's behavior. He simply walks through, and Matthew calls for quiet. Jesus tells him, "Peace be with you." Then Matthew thanks Jesus for coming to his house.

I had lived under a fallacy for most of my life, thinking only wretched sinners hung out in such dens of iniquity. What a start when I realized that Matthew was the kind of person Jesus was recruiting into his inner circle—a person who was living in the world, surrounded by people of the world! Upon more reflection, I realized that Jesus never elevated himself above anyone like Matthew; he didn't see Matthew as evil or his gathering as a forbidden place. Jesus knew he needed to be in contact with the people of the world, people who could cleave to him and start afresh. In Matthew, Jesus found someone not tied to old rituals and habits, but open to the profound new message of salvation. Matthew was able to connect to his world and could make his ministry relevant to his people. He could pilot his life through the world as it was, a world full of brokenness but ready for redemption, just as he had been.

How is it that this is not a principle we live? In one of his books, C. Pete Wagner notes that the first two years of any Christian's life is the period with the most potential for spreading the gospel. At that time, most of the new believer's friends are still living in the world, and he or she still maintains those friendships. But as time passes, the new believer is swept into the church and loses contact with old friends in the world. Despite the example of Jesus, somehow the church continues to model that the only safe place in this world is inside the church with those who are redeemed.

I was raised in a church that took this belief in sequestering ourselves as far as possible. As matter of fact, we tried to remove ourselves from other churches because we were afraid of being soiled or contaminated by their practices and beliefs. We were told that by hanging around with others outside of the fold, sooner or later we would be practicing the deeds of these individuals who had less faith than we did. But over time, I have seen that that type of thinking is highly flawed. Seclusion is no safeguard from evil. Adam and Eve proved that in the very first book of the Bible. They were God's new creation, free of sin, completely pure. They lived in a garden paradise that provided all they could ever need or want. Yet they still found a way to transgress and eat the fruit from the Tree of Knowledge. In this ideal environment, they still missed the mark.

In our own story of creation, at the forefront is the idea that being in the right environment will not protect you from making mistakes. Then, in the coming of Jesus and his plan for salvation, we are taught that we are all sinners and that those sins are redeemed through him. It seems to me that seclusion is a human invention and not one modeled by Jesus, considering the fact that Jesus did not fear the world, nor did he shun it. And time and time again, seclusion proves an ineffective tool to protect people from evil. I know from personal experience that refraining from the world was the reason I developed a dual personality, where I did what I wanted despite the precepts of my church and just hoped I didn't get caught. I saw with my own children that sending them to Christian schools didn't keep them from breaking the rules. Over time, it became clear to me that all we were accomplishing in our attempt to be pure was maintaining an appearance. That pretense was to make our own group feel holy and pure and "in."

I used to teach about this very principle of seclusion—in support of it—using the example of Noah and the ark. The flood was coming, I would say, and the only place to be safe was in the ark. The flood represented the outside world, and the ark represented God's protection from the destruction at hand. I look back and think that I misunderstood so much. We are not fighting against people or culture. In fact, the very reason Jesus came to the planet was to infiltrate our lives, not to isolate himself from our humanity or brokenness. He wasn't afraid of being contaminated by the world, nor did he teach that philosophy to those who followed him.

In his life and ministry, Jesus didn't adhere to the religious wisdom of his day.

He didn't act, think, or look like the other rabbis. Instead, he engaged with the lepers of his day, both literal and figurative. He gravitated toward people who were considered the lowest and most unholy, people who were down and out, people the sacred groups refused to touch or incorporate. Jesus broke the mold; he refused to be placed in a niche group where he could be easily identified by his dress or speech or behavior. He wasn't Pentecostal, Lutheran, Catholic, or Methodist. He wasn't independent or libertarian, conservative or liberal. He wasn't a Pharisee or a Sadducee. He maintained his own identity that allowed him to move in and out of groups without being tied to a set of policies. Refusing to toe the line, Jesus defined himself instead of being defined by the religious institutions of his time. In fact, he spoke of a truth that transcended the religious institutions.

As I have said before, I was taught, both by word and example, that we should be separate from the culture. For most of my life, that is how I lived, surrounded by people who thought and looked and acted like me. Now, I believe this seclusion has two effects. One, it builds walls between people in the church and people outside of it, and the two groups do not relate to one another on a personal level but as stereotypes. Christians begin seeing the people outside the church as lost, maybe dangerous, potentially evil. According to George Barna's polls, people who don't go to church also have a view of people who do: that they are far more judgmental than the general population. If we are honest with ourselves, we shouldn't deny it. As Christians, we are taught from early on that we know who is saved and who is unsaved. We believe that we have the only truth, and that if people don't accept our truth, they are damned to hell. The church proclaims itself as a place where the holy meet, as a fortress against everyone else.

Of course, this is contradicted in Scripture, in the example that Jesus gives us about the tares and the wheat. He says, "The tares and the wheat are all together, and you don't know the difference." Tares and wheat look identical, but when you break open a grain of wheat, you'll find a kernel; and in the tares, you won't. Like in the book of Samuel, Jesus is saying, "Man looks on the outside, but God looks on the heart." As humans, we don't even see the right things.

We judge anyway, and we do it because it makes us feel safe and strong. Yet we don't realize we are wielding a double-edged sword, which cuts at those we judge and paradoxically cuts at ourselves. My own judgment made real the verse in Matthew: "Judge not, lest ye be judged." It's hard to put into words, but the judgment I wielded made me hate the things about myself that weren't perfect.

After decades of harboring judgment about myself and everyone around me, I was deeply wounded.

Unexpectedly, my healing came in the form of knowing individuals outside of the church. I had always felt a little more comfortable around those people because I could be myself. It seemed like I could have normal conversations with them. We could be honest about what music we liked or that we enjoyed having a few drinks; or later on in life, about what was happening in our marriages, with our finances, with our kids. We could be real. It was such a striking contrast to relationships we had at church, where we had to walk in with a smile on our faces, and we couldn't talk about the real issues because it would break the image of the perfect and victorious life in Jesus.

Another time where I felt a lot of healing was the first time I went to a professional counselor. It felt so comforting, because I could say exactly what was going on—troubles with my faith and my marriage and my career as a pastor—and I didn't have to worry about being judged. If I had shared the same things with someone in the church, they would have come back with a prescription: I needed to pray harder or have more faith or trust. It always came back to a flaw in you—if your faith was stronger, you wouldn't be having this type of problem. With the counselor, I just got to say it, and I didn't get back any judgment. I felt accepted.

But the most important moment of healing was when I realized that God was working in people outside of the church, and that he was doing things without my help, without my permission, and certainly despite my judgment. Around 2004, Canyon View Vineyard began a new ministry, opening free medical clinics in Grand Junction. Spearheaded by a nurse who attended our church, we rented buildings away from the church facility, and we set up clinics to perform blood tests for diabetes, eye screening, and such common procedures as taking a person's blood pressure. Volunteers from the medical community came out of the woodwork to share their skills with people in need.

Between the doctors, nurses, and technicians, there were probably sixty or seventy medical personnel coming to volunteer at the clinics, which we would hold as often as our resources allowed us. These people worked hard and lived for the weekends, but they gave up time they could have been spending any way they chose. Some of the volunteers were from our church; others were not believers at all but were willing to give their weekends or afternoons to help people who were hurting. One Catholic woman volunteered with us, undeterred by the fact that we weren't Catholic. She believed God had gifted her with skills to help people, and she was glad for the opportunity to give to people in need. And though the work was basic care, they truly were saving people's lives. I remember in one case, they tested a man's sugar levels and found them to be off the charts—he didn't know he was diabetic. Because of that test, they got him to the hospital, and they saved his life.

Truly, these volunteers weren't there for recognition or to build their practices. They just wanted to help their fellow human beings. Many of these people weren't professed Christians and didn't live a lifestyle that would be easily recognized as traditionally Christian—they didn't necessarily attend church regularly or go to Bible study or tithe their 10 percent—but they had a heart of compassion. Some of the greatest touches of human kindness I have ever witnessed happened at the hands of these doctors and nurses at our free medical clinic.

That's when I began to understand what Jesus was doing with Matthew. That's when I had a revelation: that God was already working, and that he was touching people in ways that were often superior to what we were doing. I realized that, in some instances, he was using people outside the church to show his love better than we were as Christians.

I had always known that God was with the unchurched, at least intellectually. I used to ask my congregations who God loved more, those inside or outside the church. We all knew the answer: that God loved them both the same. What I didn't realize was that those outside the church were demonstrating his love in real ways. They were doing God's work without even knowing it was God's work.

The more I watched, the more I saw that was Christlike in their service. These doctors and nurses weren't looking for credit. They didn't want their names in the church bulletin or in the local paper. Jesus said, "Let your giving be behind closed doors. Don't let your good deeds be known before men." When I saw these people helping, it was the purest form of giving, because they weren't advertising it, and they didn't want anything from it.

Another thing I noticed that was Christlike was that they were accepting of each other and their patients. They didn't have barriers, and they didn't try to dig into a patient's past to change him or her before they would offer help. Now that I am working with hospice, I see the same thing. Social workers and nurses don't ask if their patients are Buddhist or Christian or what their philosophy of life is. They don't care about the person's lifestyle or who the person is sleeping with. They help the person without condition, which is the same way Jesus operated.

He dined with the tax collector, which would have constituted ritual impurity, then he went even further by asking for a drink from the Samaritan woman at the well. In Jesus's time, people who were afflicted—with blindness, with leprosy, with paralysis, with epilepsy—were supposedly that way because of their sins, but Jesus didn't ask them a list of questions before he healed them. He did it unconditionally.

My experience with the medical clinic prompted me to do a lot of reflection and soul-searching. Why were these people, many of whom had no training in the church, exhibiting characteristics that were like Christ? Why did their love seem more natural and less of an effort than it was for me, who had been a practicing Christian for a number of years? I was surprised to find that they seemingly had more peace in their lives than I did in mine. It was shocking that where they were manifesting love, my tendency was criticism and judgment. I was more frustrated. I had less contentment. I was angrier.

I turned this over in my mind for some time, and I finally realized that these unchurched people were teaching me. Through their example, I realized what it meant to practice acts of compassion with no ulterior motive, how to accept and love people unconditionally, and finally—and this is one of the most liberating things I have ever discovered—*that judging people is much harder than loving them.* I learned that what Jesus called us to do—to love one another—is an easy yoke, as he promised.

I wonder sometimes at our audacity with judgment. For so much of my life, I felt I had to judge everyone around me to see if they were abiding by the rules of the club. That's what everyone else was doing. The examples from my childhood are extreme, but honestly, when you look at the old churches, where women wore their hair in buns on the tops of their heads and their dresses two inches below their knees—as if it were holy to have buns on the top of their heads and their dresses two inches below their knees—really, these rules were not anything more than a way for people to show that they were part of these little clubs that humans have designed along the way. A rule is made because the leader has a conviction one day about the length of a dress or some other action or behavior. Once they build up enough rules, the sect becomes distinct and the rules become a way to designate whether you are in the club or not. It becomes very easy to tell when someone is not fitting in, when someone is not "saved."

Yet how could we ever know? Most of our policies and regulations have to do with external appearances, not with conditions of the heart. How easily we forget about the tares and the wheat, and that man looks on the outward appearance but God looks on the heart. How often we ignore what Jesus says in the Gospel of Luke, chapter 6: "Stop judging and you will not be judged. Stop condemning and you will not be condemned. Forgive and you will be forgiven. Give and gifts will be given to you; a good measure, packed together, shaken down and overflowing, will be poured into your lap. For the measure with which you measure will in turn be measured out to you." What you do to others will be your fate. As humans, we cannot see clearly; we are the blind leading the blind. We are not the teacher. "Why do you notice the splinter in your brother's eye, but do not perceive the wooden beam in your own?" Jesus asks. We should be worried about our own hearts, rather than judging our neighbors.

Those hoops you have to jump through to be able to categorize and condemn people, to build those barriers between you and another person, are exhausting. I realized that when I stopped judging, I was able to stop worrying about whether a person was going to change his lifestyle so he could fit in with the church, and I could just be his friend. Then I began to feel a sense of sorrow for the people who were constantly being judged. I hurt for them because I knew they would never be accepted by the church, that if they ever started going to church and began to open up about who they were, they'd be rejected. If we truly want people to be a part of the church, we have find a way to accept people where they are, not expect them to be something else.

The more I have settled into this practice of loving instead of judging, the more certain I am of it. In my experience, God has never asked my opinion about someone else's lifestyle. He did not ask me or any other human being to designate whether someone's lifestyle is right or wrong. He only asks me to accept my broken brothers and sisters with compassion, the way I need to accept my broken self.

At this point in human history, most people know what Christians believe. Especially in the Western world, it would be difficult for someone to go through life without hearing the story of Jesus—of his miraculous birth, the radical lessons he taught, like turning the other cheek, and the hopeful message about his triumph over sin and death. But somewhere along the way, the sad fact that really began to penetrate my heart was that the unchurched know more about what we believe than they know about our love.

I had always heard that the church is called to be salt to the world w…
If we think about it, salt only has value upon contact, when it touches the meat
or vegetables or potatoes and highlights the distinctive characteristics of the food.
Salt has absolutely no effect on a piece of meat when the two never meet. So the
church must be a part of the world, in full contact with all of God's creation in
order to impact the world. Isolated from the world, we cannot love the world.
Isolated from the world, Christians appear to the world as judgmental and nar-
row-minded. Isolated from the world, the salt cannot add flavor.

Recently, I have begun thinking about how it is not only the food that under-
goes a change when it comes in contact with salt. Salt isn't palatable on its own;
like with meat, the strengths of the salt are highlighted in the interaction. Applying
this metaphor to my own life, how much did I miss by labeling people like
Matthew and gatherings like his a forbidden zone?

Jesus was drawn toward people who were streetwise, who knew that life was
difficult and complicated, and who, once they met him, knew that they had found
truth. Some of the most moving stories in the New Testament are moments when
this happens, like when the sinful woman washes Jesus's feet with her tears and
anoints them with oil. I think that's why I love that scene at Matthew's house in
Jesus of Nazareth so much. That party has about every debauched thing you can
imagine happening. But there's a shot of Jesus, smiling and serene amid all of it.
When I saw that, I thought, *That's it. That's how Christianity should be lived, in the
midst of people.*

That doesn't mean that Jesus was carousing and becoming drunk and com-
promising himself. He knew who he was, and he maintained who he was while
being a part of the world. One way to think about the way Jesus was versus the
way the church exists in the world today is the difference between being *insulated*
and being *isolated*. The church isolates itself; it cuts itself off from the world in
order to protect itself. But Jesus was insulated. He was a part of the world but not
affected by the world. He was in the culture, but the culture didn't penetrate his
values—it didn't change him.

But as Matthew says to Simon Peter in *Jesus of Nazareth*, after knowing Jesus,
"We'll never be the same, and neither will anyone in the whole world."

If Christians truly want to impact the world, we have to be in the world lov-
ingly and without judgment. It's important to take the model that Jesus gave us
and learn how to work within the culture to show God's love without losing ourselves. We should be teaching young believers in a way that makes them want to

cling to Jesus when they get out into the world and are given the opportunity to make a choice. We should be building strong inner lives that are impervious to the temptations of the flesh, insulating ourselves by knowing what our own values are, how our own faith guides us, and in a practical sense, knowing what is good for our bodies and spirits.

I think one reason this isn't the way we train believers is that it is more involved than what we actually do. In the same way that it's easier to teach rote memorization than to help someone learn to think critically, it's easier to isolate than to insulate. By secluding ourselves, we think there's less risk of being tempted or having to use our willpower to resist behaviors that go against our moral compass. But that lifestyle is a contrast to the way our Savior lived, and here again, I'll bring up the story of Adam and Eve to remind us that seclusion is not foolproof. I think we have to ask ourselves, are we most concerned with maintaining that lifestyle and showing that we are morally superior? Or are we going to reach out to the world to show God's love?

In my mind, the answer to the first question should be, "Absolutely not." We are not trying to win an intellectual argument that our lifestyle is superior. In my mind, the answer to the second question is, "Yes, absolutely." We are called to be light to the world, to share the good news, to mirror the love of the Father and the Son. And getting someone to change their lifestyle is not the goal of loving people. The end result of loving others is that you love them. In the last few years, I have found that love has so much more benefit, both to me and to others, than trying to win an intellectual argument. I have found that loving people builds more bridges than judging them or trying to change them. I have found that loving people helps me accept myself. And our perfect model—the model of Jesus—is the model of love. If that's the path he took, I think it's a pretty good example to follow.

I feel so energized when I reflect on being with people anywhere, in any place, belief system, or circumstance, and realize this is what Jesus did.

He related to people where they were.

His lifestyle made him fluid, flexible, and adaptable.

He didn't give up who he was and adopt the behaviors of those around him, but he connected with his fellow human beings.

In everything he did and taught, he was relevant.

The church sometimes can be so out of touch with society. We're always wishing that things would go back to an idealized past, lamenting the immorality of the current day and trying to get as far from it as possible. But I don't see this in the Lord's life as he traversed our planet, though there were many immoral things happening even then. There was something about his message that was so attractive that scores of people from all walks of life wanted to hear what he had to say. Remember, many of these people had heard what their religious leaders were teaching. Suddenly this Jesus came along, and what he was saying and doing was what impacted their lives.

One of the most revolutionary traits in Jesus was that he embraced these people in their humanity—that he embraced humanity instead of condemning us, both by becoming human and by loving us as humans. At the Last Supper, Jesus takes the bread and breaks it, and he says, "This is my body, broken for you." One way I read that is that Jesus is saying, "I identify with your brokenness." That's why he came, and that's why he died. He is saying, "I am identifying with that part of you that will always be broken because human beings are broken."

In the Psalms, it says, "We are but dust." We are weak. We are not going to live up to some impossible standard. In the church, there is lip service paid to how we are depraved and weak, but it seems that we talk about accepting our humanity more than we practice it.

So what if we change how we think?

What if we think of a communion service as an opportunity to celebrate our brokenness, to accept it? To remind ourselves that someday we will be whole, but it will probably not to be today, or this week, or even this decade?

And if we accept that in ourselves, maybe we'll allow other people to be human as well.

We'll stop trying to clean the fish before we catch it.

Maybe we'll even realize that catching the fish isn't all on our shoulders, and that God is always working in his people, even without our knowledge or permission.

CHAPTER 10

BREAKING THE MOLD

When I was in the seventh grade, my parents asked me if I was ready to be baptized. For a few months, it seemed like baptism had been looming on the horizon, as one of my peers and then another was dunked in the font at the front of the church. Though it was unspoken, there was pressure building for me to do the same. My mom reinforced it when she told me that my cousin had decided to be baptized.

So I answered, *Yes*, I was ready to be baptized.

I wasn't an idiot; I picked up on their cues. I knew this was something they wanted me to do. I knew that it was more their desire than my own, that it was something I was doing because everybody else was doing it rather than because it was something I wanted in my own heart. At the time, the ritual of baptism did not mean a great deal to me. In fact, I can't say that I really understood what it meant at all. First and foremost, I was being obedient—to my church and my parents—rather than understanding what baptism was all about.

After I said yes, one Sunday I found myself at the rectangular tank used for baptisms behind the altar. On the wall above it was a painted landscape of mountains. I felt nervous, not because of any significance I tied to baptism, but because I had to share a little testimony with the few hundred people in the congregation like everyone else when they got baptized; and like everyone else, I mumbled something about having sinned, about thanking Jesus, about wanting to live for him. Then the preacher dunked me, and I came up chilled and wet and relieved that it was over.

A few years later, I found myself with some friends on a bridge outside of town. The superstructure reached far above the road but was easy to scale, and from the topmost point, the river swirled about sixty feet below. With all my friends watching, and to prove myself to them, I climbed the bridge and jumped. I was terrified; I had a significant fear of heights that normally would have kept me from such reckless behavior. There is no way I would ever have done it on my own, but that day, to make sure that the group accepted me, to make sure everyone knew I was "cool," I overcame my phobia and jumped off the bridge.

These two events obviously differed in degree and in consequence. Being dunked in a baptismal font did not carry the same danger as jumping off a sixty-foot bridge. But the thing that strikes me is how closely they resemble one another in kind—that I was motived by what others thought rather than my own will. I chose to be baptized to please the people around me and because all of my friends were doing it; I chose to jump off the bridge for the same reason.

I have lived much of my life in the same way, always allowing my environment to exert enormous pressure on me. It makes me sad to realize that my internal compass wasn't stronger, that I wasn't able to allow my own discernment to guide my actions, that instead, I deferred to the group. But truthfully, I was never taught that personal convictions were more important than group standards. For so long, others told me what was right and what was wrong; if my own conscience tried to break in, I couldn't even hear it. I never learned how to use my God-given discernment, my common sense, and my conscience to make choices, to make sure that the path I was following was guided by the truth at the core of my being. I think that this, more than anything else, prevented me from becoming a mature, fully developed Christian man.

In the 1970s, a pastor in South America named Juan Carlos Ortiz wrote about the challenges of discipleship. In his book *Disciple,* he describes the criticism he faced for a new direction in his ministry, where, instead of staying inside the church walls, Ortiz began going to cocktail parties and other places that weren't sanctioned Christian events. His purpose was to do what Christ did—to infiltrate the world where people were living, to give them hope and a light. But almost immediately, he was bombarded by other Christians with criticism for subjecting himself to bad influences and for opening himself up to temptation.

This reaction made him made him question why the church wasn't maturing people to a place where they could understand that this was exactly what Christ did. Why was it that church structures were not helping people develop in Christ so that it was internal strength, not external pressure, that won out? His idea was that the church creates—and he doesn't use these words, but I do—an atmosphere of codependency. One person does all the thinking: these are the guidelines, this is how you live your Christian life. The decisions are already made, regardless of the individual. You are not to go to that party, the leader says, even if you don't think you are going to be tempted to do things that would go against your conscience.

Because what if you take a wrong step? What if you mess up? It's better not to chance it and make sure you are on the right path.

What Ortiz argued was that these sanctions don't allow people to mature. They can't judge for themselves what they should or shouldn't do, or what their faith means to them, or what form their faith should take. Ortiz called this the "eternal childhood of the believer."

In my own life, I experienced a form of this. For three decades, I had been doing all the things I had been taught, thinking that if I prayed, read the Bible, worshiped, tithed—if I did all these disciplines—I would grow up. I would become a mature and fully-formed Christian. But that was not the effect. Those things on their own were not a magic formula.

I didn't realize this for a long time, until I went to see a professional counselor after my life was falling apart. She helped me understand that the only source I had for understanding the world was my childhood church. I realized that I couldn't think outside the box. I couldn't question God. I couldn't question marriage. I couldn't question prayer. I couldn't question church. I couldn't work through the different issues that came up because then I would appear disloyal. I realized that my life had been predetermined by the shape of my religious upbringing, and I had not developed the internal fortitude to work things out on my own. And finally, I realized that I held a certain amount of resentment toward the church because I had bought into a conviction that was theirs but not mine.

How thin was my faith because of this? I wondered.

And how easily shattered.

At this point, I should say that I do think young believers need instruction. Young believers need guidance to learn about the Father, Son, and Holy Spirit, to learn about Scripture and prayer and the loving sacrifice of Jesus Christ that redeemed the world. It is right and good to help people who are seeking God in their journey.

But at some point, individuals must assume responsibility for their faith and discover their own personal belief system that will help them navigate their lives. They may never leave the church of their childhood, but at some point, each individual must examine what was put into the box and then figure out what is right for him or her. Discarding some parts and holding on to others is our spiritual pilgrimage, where we learn about who we are with God.

In this process, there is an inherent tension. I think this is one reason why organizations are so inflexible: they feel that if you let people follow their own path, everything will descend into chaos. If there is no standard interpretation of Scripture, then it's a free-for-all on what it says to you and what it says to me—soon, we may have thousands of interpretations of the same phrase.

For people who say that asking questions or doubting certain parts of Christian orthodoxy leads down a path to evil, or unbelief, or relativism, or unorthodox interpretations, my response centers on my new understanding of this merciful and magnanimous God and his love for his people. I believe that if individuals are really honest in their questions and are seeking truth, they're going to be okay. God's got really big shoulders. Instead of demonizing it, I have come to believe that this questioning and self-discovery is important, and after a period of basic instruction, believers must leave the elementary things behind. We must develop our own walks with God. We must find answers that resonate with our own hearts. We must find frameworks that mirror the closely held convictions that emanate from the core of each one of us, convictions that develop through our experiences both with God and with humanity. And we must allow our brothers and sisters to make their own way as well.

How much do we allow the church to be that inclusive place?

How often does the church accept people with all their faults, all their brokenness, all their humanity?

How often do we truly have patience to allow people to change, to find their own way, to discover their own walk with God? How often do we relax and tell ourselves, "That person's exploration is not a threat"?

In my experience, it's more of an exception than the rule.

Of course, it could be argued that there are always new sects popping up whose beliefs are more lenient, and that they offer different perspectives on what it means to be a Christian and challenges to certain orthodox ideas. And I would certainly never argue that Christians should all be painted with the same brush. I actually believe that's been done for far too long, to the detriment of Christianity.

In my experience, however, the moment a new movement solidifies into an organization, something changes. Almost immediately, a tension between the individual and the institution arises. Of course, this seems to be the case with any institution, whether it's religious or secular. Even something as simple as living in a city means you give up certain individual freedoms for the good of the collective; you can't allow your dog to run off-leash as you might in a rural area,

for example. With regard to religion, things aren't that different. /
code of conduct and profess the beliefs of the church that we cho/

But in the many years I have watched different churches come ᵢ……
and evolve, I have noticed a pattern. It seems to me that the degree to which we
abdicate our own personal freedom is often in direct proportion to the pull of
gravity that the organization has—how much influence it has on the way you
live your everyday life. A church like the one I grew up in had a lot of pull. There
were very clear-cut beliefs and a list of acceptable behaviors, and there was very
little leeway for individual expression. They did not tolerate discussion about
doctrinal matters, like whether Christians would be taken before or after the Trials
and Tribulations; the answer was, of course, we would be taken away before that
occurred, without question. As for behavior, when you joined the church, you
signed a membership card that said you wouldn't go to dances or to the movies.

If that sounds too outmoded to be relevant, in the last couple years, a
megachurch in Washington, whose pastor preaches against "sinning through questioning," made headlines for the amount of control it exerts over its members'
lives, particularly their sex lives. Upon joining, members sign a "covenant" in
which they agree to refrain from sinful behavior "as the Bible, my pastors, and my
conscience dictate." (It's interesting to note that even in their "covenant," the individual is mentioned only after the pastors, who uphold the values of the institution.) And if the member breaks the covenant, the church has discipline policies.

Nowadays, there's also a political element that seems to go along with being
a Christian, and toeing the line means abiding by the social values and political
paradigm set by Jerry Falwell and his Moral Majority in 1979. Increasingly, there
is obvious hostility toward those who don't subscribe to the teaching of the group.
There is no room for conversation or even polite tolerance for someone with a
different point of view, and I believe this has hurt the church in two ways: one,
by creating more of a separation between the church and the more secular and
liberal parts of the culture, and two, by pigeonholing all Christians into certain
beliefs, not allowing them to really figure out their own stances through discussion
and exploration. I see it as a failing that we have abdicated all of our thoughts
and ideas and opinions to the Republican Party.

It is true that often religion and public policy overlap, and we should all be
engaged in politics in a way that honors our faith. But requiring all Christians to
be social conservatives is quite close to the rigid fundamentalist upbringing of
my childhood, where we were told what to believe in all aspects of our lives. At

Canyon View Vineyard, I regularly had to tell people that we would not be pigeonholed as a right-wing church. It wasn't because I disagreed with conservative philosophies as much as that I believed there should be space for people who had different views to come and be a part of a Christian community. As someone who had a heart for the unchurched, I hoped that we could attract people who were Democrats and people who didn't ascribe to hard-and-fast political views. Yet time and time again, I would see people ostracized for being open to a different political point of view. If someone even broached the subject of abortion or another controversial topic, that conversation would be completely cut off. Over a period of time, I would see that person being ostracized from the group because they didn't fit in politically.

There are a few different reasons I think it is a problem to require every Christian to have all the same convictions and opinions, and for the political discourse to be so inflexible. First of all, it prevents people from really getting to the heart of each issue, finding information that really compels them, and making a judgment based on their own consciences. This in turn makes the belief shakier, since the person didn't come to his or her own conclusion. (It's like the foreclosed identity, where the belief is not internalized as much as when an individual really wrestles with an issue and comes to a place of belief himself.)

Second, it's healthy and biblical to have a fervent discourse. "As iron sharpens iron, so one man's countenance the countenance of another," says the old proverb.

Third, it divides things sharply into black and white, and that's well and good until the reality of life sets in and you realize that things are gray. For example, people feel very strongly about the right to life. Yet in hospice, I often work with people who have a terminally ill loved one on life support, and they pause because things become a little gray. They may ask themselves, "What qualifies as life? Would this person be alive today if it weren't for our modern medicine?"

To be clear, I am not espousing Kevorkian beliefs or belittling the right-to-life movement, which I do support. But I think we have to have the discussion. We, as a civilized people, need to have the discussion. Life pushes people in the gray areas all the time, and then they are on their own because we can't have the discussion in the church. It's a journey to figure this life out, a journey riddled with doubt and questions and many, many mistakes on our part. But in the Bible, I see places where God allows questioning and dissent, and he also allows humans to have different opinions, and he meets them where they are, if they fall down or if they fail.

In Genesis, Abraham pleads for the city Sodom. "Will you sweep away the righteous with the wicked?" he asks God. "What if there are fifty righteous people in the city? Will you really sweep it away and not spare the place for the sake of the fifty righteous people in it? Far be it from you to do such a thing—to kill the righteous with the wicked, treating the righteous and the wicked alike. Far be it from you! Will not the Judge of all the earth do right?"

The Lord does not chastise Abraham for his questions. Instead, the Lord assents: "If I find fifty righteous people in the city of Sodom, I will spare the whole place for their sake."

Abraham does not stop there. "Now that I have been so bold as to speak to the Lord," he says, "though I am nothing but dust and ashes, what if the number of the righteous is five less than fifty? Will you destroy the whole city for lack of five people?"

"If I find forty-five there," God says, "I will not destroy it."

Abraham continues with forty, thirty, twenty, even down to ten, and each time, God tolerates Abraham's challenge and replies with mercy.

It happens again in the first chapter of Isaiah, when the Lord says, "Come now, let us reason together. Though your sins are like scarlet, they shall be as white as snow; though they are red as crimson, they shall be like wool." This happens in the midst of the Israelites turning away from him, in their rejection of his law. But God is open; he is asking his people, "How can we reconcile?"

Another illustration is when Isaiah goes in to prophesy to King Hezekiah, saying, "Set your house in order, for you shall die; you shall not recover." And it says that King Hezekiah turned his face toward the wall and wept bitterly. As Isaiah went out into the courtyard, God spoke to him and said, "Go back in and tell him that he has fifteen more years." In the moment, God changes his mind and says, "Okay. I'll deal with you on that level."

Another compromise occurs in the New Testament. After the resurrection, Jesus appears to Peter while he's out fishing on the Sea of Galilee. Peter strips down and jumps into the water. When Peter reaches where Jesus is, Jesus asks him, "Peter, do you love me?" The first time, Jesus uses *agape*—unconditional, almost divine love.

Peter answers, "Lord, you know I love you." But he uses *philia,* the word for human, fraternal, imperfect love.

Again, Jesus asks, "Peter, do you love me?" *Agape.*

Peter answers, "Lord, you know I love you"—*philia.*

Finally the third time, Jesus asks, "Peter, do you love me?" And this time he uses *philia*.

Peter answers, "That's the kind of love I can love you with."

So Jesus changes his standard. Instead of rigidity, there is mercy, there is grace, and there is an acceptance of the imperfect human.

It seems to me that Jesus wanted people to work through the complexities of faith, and he accepted people where they were in that process.

He taught in parables, which are not straightforward or obvious; instead, they required the listener to really delve in and think critically to untie the knot.

He also often answered people's questions with questions: "What do you think? What do you believe?"

I believe that to follow the true example of Christ, we have to be willing to do the same.

I have the confidence to say these things now, but not without a heavy heart for how long it took me to get here. I saw people I grew up with leaving the church, people who resisted the emotionalism and the rigidity and the groupthink and said, "I'm not buying it." Some of them left as soon as they were eighteen. They were done. The judgment that fell on them was, "Well, we know where they are going." And I wasn't innocent of that judgment.

When my own children began questioning religion when they were teenagers, I was angry and wished they would just fall in line. At the time, I thought their questioning was risky for several reasons. I worried that they would engage in harmful behaviors, and that if they fell away from the Christian faith they would jeopardize their salvation. But I can't deny that I was also worried it would reflect poorly on me as the pastor to have a child who didn't follow the rules, who didn't completely buy in.

When I look back, I really admire those people who were willing to admit they had questions. Some people seem to transcend the organization; for one reason or another in their hearts, they say, *This isn't for me.* In my many years as a pastor, I met a lot of these people who passed through, and even when we were the latest, greatest thing going in Grand Junction, and thousands of people were joining up as members of Canyon View Vineyard, we still didn't meet their needs. That was hard for me. Without realizing it, I wanted them to stick around, to engage in groupthink. And they were saying, "No, it's not for me." Now I realize they were light-years ahead of me in their relationship with God.

I admire that they had the courage to look for a different path; I wish I'd had the guts to do the same. Because when people find their own way, it seems to be an authentic, honest, and heartfelt existence. It seems like they know themselves—they are very aware of themselves, their needs, and what they believe. They are building their own lives rather than living inside a fence built by someone else.

I was never taught how much freedom would be available to me when I began discovering and living my own convictions. I never realized how good it would feel when I could speak from my heart about those convictions, when the answers I was giving came out of my own experience rather than something I repeated because my pastor had said it. I always had a blind type of faith, and one with very rigid boundaries. Only recently have I discovered that my mind and my faith can actually work together, especially at times when the black-and-white answer doesn't seem to leave any room for mercy or allow any exception to the rule. Now I use my common sense to help me through a gray area in life, and I am comfortable with the fact that the boundaries need to have some give. And this is not without biblical precedent. In certain instances, Jesus overrides the law when the law will do more harm than good. In the second chapter of Mark, Jesus is walking through the grain fields with his disciples on the Sabbath, and the disciples, who are hungry, begin picking some heads of grain. The Pharisees ask him why they are breaking the law against working on the Sabbath.

Jesus answers them, "Have you never read what David did when he and his companions were hungry and in need? In the days of Abiathar the high priest, he entered the house of God and ate the consecrated bread, which is lawful only for priests to eat. And he also gave some to his companions." The law was not absolute, Jesus was saying. There are exceptions. Picking the grain was a practical solution for the disciples' hunger, as was eating the consecrated bread for David.

In both cases, common sense gave directions to his actions. Sometimes common sense is the practical guide to solving the dilemmas in our lives. Why do we discount this tool? If there is a biblical precedent for overriding our legalism, why do we refuse it? If common sense was a guide for David and for Jesus, could it be that guide is as divine as a prescription to keep holy the Sabbath?

And what of what Jesus said next? "The Sabbath was made for man, not man for the Sabbath." Here, Jesus is emphasizing the ethical, in his typical fashion. He is saying that God gave us the Sabbath because we needed the Sabbath—because we needed to be reminded to rest, and we needed to be reminded to give God thanks and praise for our blessings. But God did not ask us to starve because of it. The legalism that developed with the Pharisees about keeping the Sabbath—how it was keeping the Sabbath to take fifty paces, but fifty-one would be sinful—is mistaking the letter of the law for the spirit of it. We can see that clearly in looking back at the Pharisees, but how often do we step outside our own religious framework and look at our teachings through the eyes of those searching for faith? Why can't we be self-aware and reflective enough to recognize that we are the ones tying up heavy burdens and laying them across people's shoulders? How heavy is it carrying someone else's convictions? How heavy and empty to live a life designed by someone else's rules?

The faith I practice now has greater meaning to me because I'm learning what my beliefs are and what I practice that forms my convictions. I feel free to be who I am, to be who I have always wanted to be, rather than denying myself to fit a mold. I have finally discovered what I feel to be the truth in John 8:36: "So if the Son sets you free, you will be free indeed." I have been freed of my legalism, freed of my judgment of others. I am free to love the people in the world and to live richly, and I am so grateful to have traded the heavy yoke for the one that Christ promised, the one that is easy and light.

I no longer feel the need to stop a debate if it is wandering out of orthodox Christian bounds. I will be there to listen and engage, but I don't feel the pressure to change a person's mind or lifestyle. After many years of using my words to try to win an argument or persuade someone to say the sinner's prayer, I've realized that if there is really going to be a change, it's not going to be because of anything I say or do. It will be because there is an inner conviction, one brought about by God himself.

As I explained in the last chapter, recognizing that God was working without my knowledge or permission was incredibly liberating. It relieved me of the burden—and the arrogance—of thinking I had to do it all. In the last few years, I've been blessed to see that many people outside the church have a relationship with God, and they honor God in the way they live. Working in a hospice center has taught me that there are a lot of people who are truly spiritual who have never gone to church. I see my colleagues giving their lives for the people around them, living compassionate and sacrificial lives, though it's not how any church has prescribed it. They might be people who, for one reason or another, have always resisted the established order. Maybe that's how their brains are wired. because the established order rejected who they were. But that doesn't make them evil or wrong. They are living their consciences and are learning by life experience. And it's been pivotal for me to realize that God loves these individuals and is working in their lives.

With many of the patients and their families, the same thing is true. One of the things that I love about hospice patients is their honesty. They are close to death, and they have abandoned most of the pretense. Many of them will say, "I believe that there is a hereafter, but I don't know how it happens or what form it takes." There is something so refreshing and so honest, rather than saying they know for certain—when they can't say that truthfully. In my estimation, for people to ask and continue asking really breeds a dialogue and an honesty with God.

I am humbled by what I see around me, by the depth and breadth of what it means to face death, and by how humans can reach out to one another to extend comfort and compassion. I feel so blessed to be a part, however small, of that process.

It's a radical vision of the church: to allow people to think and act and be who they want to be, to suspend judgment and give them time and space to explore and find God for themselves. I'm sure that if that happened, the church establishment would begin their cries of relativism and claims that letting people push the boundaries will lead to sin and all manner of behavior and belief.

But this is not a new claim—it has been made every time any institution faced dissent. And if we truly believe that questioning and exploration will lead to destruction, then where is our belief in God's sovereignty? Where is our faith that God is a powerful and loving force who guides our lives and redeems all things?

It seems to me that being open and loving, treating people with kindness and giving them the grace that God has promised, is what our example is in Christ. So I try to practice that myself. I give myself latitude to explore and discover God in the ways that seem authentic to me. And I extend that to others. It's very different from the days when I gave altar calls and counted the number of people who committed their lives to Christ; now I just try to make friends. Matthew says that Jesus was a friend, so that's my mission: to make friends and to extend any love and kindness I can to those around me. The thing is, you only become friends by spending time with someone, by listening instead of preaching, by offering acceptance instead of judgment.

I've learned so much from my position as hospice chaplain in the last few years. I have learned that the *last* thing people want is to be told how to live their lives, and that they pull away the moment they begin to feel judgment. I now try my hardest to avoid any inkling of that. And I have discovered that I have to gain the friendship of someone before they ever trust anything I have to share, whether it's about God or the role of suffering in our lives or how we discover peace. In other words, I have to prove to them that I love them, which is something I never had the time, the patience, or the conviction to do before.

Right now, some of my closest friends are my coworkers at the hospice center, and many of them live in ways that would be condemned by most Christian sects. And when I first was there, there was a barrier. These people were worried that I was going to preach to them and judge, so they kept their guard up and were reluctant to listen to what I had to say. To become their friend, I had to show them that I was a regular guy, a friend, someone who would go out to bars and be seen with them and have a beer with them.

And over time, I could see the barriers coming down. At this point, we are truly friends. We can sit together and have a drink, and they might ask what I think about God. But still, I am not there to preach to them. I may share what God has done in my life, but I will also share my doubts and my questions. And between us, the judgment is gone. I no longer feel the need to clean the fish before the catch—even needing to catch the fish is gone. That phrase doesn't even work anymore. Because I think they're already in the net. Many of them are connected to God in their own ways, and it's not for me to find out how. If they want to share it with me, that's great, but my goal now is to live by the principles of love, mercy, and forgiveness that were so integral to the ministry of Jesus.

Instead of preaching the gospel, I try to live the gospel, though I do it imperfectly. I try to allow space for people's questions and doubts. I try to accept myself and everyone around me as imperfect humans who are doing our best to get along. Paul talks about levels of believers, all the way from the infant to the mature believer who no longer needs the milk of the Word but instead should strive for the meat. To me, that means we are all on a path, and we must let people move along that path at their own pace, allowing them the space to make changes in their lives throughout that progression.

This has led me to a place where I feel like we should honor the seeking

instead of criticizing how people are doing it. We should allow them the
age: that personal, spiritual journey toward God. On a pilgrimage, people
carried on the shoulders of their leaders. They do not simply skate throug ___.n-
out any struggle. The idea of a pilgrimage is that you trudge, you make an exhaus-
tive and exhausting attempt to get somewhere, and you do it with the sweat of
your brow. At some point along the way, maybe you take a wrong step. Maybe
you make a right turn when you could have taken the left, and things would have
been a little easier. But I believe the biggest teacher is life experience. In my own
life, my mistakes have taught me so much; they're how I've learned for myself
what path to take, and that's where the mercy and grace of Christ fit in.

God is not surprised about the mistakes we make; what he's concerned about
is what we do afterward. God has wide, wide latitude, and he has a lot of mercy.

So you get it wrong—big deal. It's what you do afterward.

It's almost inherent within the system that people are going to try to push
those boundaries and make mistakes.

It's the story of Adam and Eve.

In Proverbs, it says, "For though a righteous man falls seven times, he rises
again."

And no matter how many times we fall down, no matter how many mistakes
we make or how winding the road, God's going to find a way to lead his people,
and he will also find a way to feed them. When the Israelites were out in the
desert, God showed that he could be with them in the harshest, darkest, most
barren places, even when they felt he was far away. When they were despairing
because they thought they'd taken the wrong path, God performed the longest-
standing miracle in all of the Bible: the forty years of manna.

God feeds us when we are lost and have nothing.

God leads us through the desert and the wilderness.

And if we truly believe in his sovereignty, we should feel free to break the
mold, to find our own path to him, to strike the rock and find a stream of water.

And we should be open when others need to go their own way.

PART III:

ONWARD

CHAPTER 11

MY JOURNEY AS A PASTOR

Sometimes I'm still surprised that I became a pastor.

When I was in high school and college, the idea of being a pastor never crossed my mind. As a young man, I loved sports, and if I had been raised in a different family, I might have gone into coaching, a field I still admire. But I absorbed the notion as a young man that the only "calling" in life was full-time ministry. Anything else was not as noble, not as holy, not as great as being a pastor. This was partly because of my mother's extreme piety and my father's admiration for pastors. But it was also because of the role the pastor played in our lives. The pastor stood at the front of the church, elevated to a place of power in his pulpit, and he was the unquestioned moral and religious authority. The pastor in my church had the ultimate say.

Even so, it was a process for me to accept my place as a minister. For the first few years as pastor at the Christian Life Center, I thought it was an exciting thing to dabble in, but I was still selling used cars at my father's car dealership, and I thought I'd continue there and take over the business one day. It was only after about five years of preaching that I accepted the fact that I was good at this, that people were responding to my leadership.

And when I reached that point, I realized something else: I realized that I could build something different from what I had grown up with. One of the things that really reinforced this desire was a conversation I had with a woman I'd gone to high school with. She shared a story that just turned my heart. Two Sundays in a row, she told me, she had gotten up and gotten dressed, driven to our church. But unable to force herself out of the car, she sat in the parking lot through the whole service. She was afraid to come in, afraid that I would ask her to stand up and introduce herself to everyone, afraid that she would be judged instead of accepted for the person she was. Two Sundays in a row she did this!

I couldn't believe she was so intimidated by the church. When she shared this with me, I began thinking that there must be others who felt this way, that there were others who wanted a spiritual home but felt that there was nowhere they'd be accepted.

And truly, at my core, I had wanted to minister to the unchurched since early on at YWAM, when I was overseas ministering to my peers in the counterculture. I knew that outside of our churches, people were not lost and hopeless. No, people really liked who Jesus was—that he did good and worked against injustice—but they didn't want to be judged, to be condemned, to be told to be someone else.

When it gets down to it, that was my deepest conviction, my reason for leading that church for all those years: that there were still people out there looking for relationship with God but unsure of where or how to find it.

So my vision was simple. I wanted to harness the excitement I felt with YWAM—the idea that I had finally discovered who God was, that he was welcoming me home, that I might have been a prodigal and had strayed off the well-worn path of the Christian walk, but that things were okay—and use it to create a place where people felt comfortable to come as they were.

But my vision was also grand. At some point, I did the math. In Grand Junction, there were 142 churches, and I added them up and figured that on any given Sunday, there were between twenty thousand and twenty-five thousand people in church, maybe thirty thousand on a big weekend. That meant there were over one hundred thousand people who were not going anywhere.

They were the unchurched, those without a home, who might just be hungry for what I had to offer.

Soon after I became a pastor full-time, our church adopted a new name and a new theology. I had learned of John Wimber's Vineyard Movement in 1984, but in 1987, we joined it. At that point in my life, it was the most liberated I had ever felt. I never knew you could have such a casual church before then. I never knew you could make a space that wasn't stuffy or staid, where pastors spoke like regular people, where the music was contemporary, not a relic of the 1950s. I can remember the first time I preached without a tie, and how I called my mom and dad and said, "This is going to be tough for you, but this is where I am going." It was a big deal to introduce that to Grand Junction in 1987, to have worship with guitars and drums, to allow people to be so informal, but people responded, and it was wonderful.

Our church came of age during the 1990s, the boom years of the evangelical movement. While mainline churches—the Southern Baptists, the Presbyterians, and the Catholics—were losing numbers, churches like mine were exploding. All across America, from Rick Warren's Saddleback in Los Angeles to Bill Hybels's Willow Creek in Chicago, nondenominational Bible churches were seeing huge increases in membership. Ours was no different. Each year, we had more people and needed bigger facilities, and each year, we added new ministries to serve a different niche. By the end of the decade, the church seemed big and vibrant and steady enough to warrant a brand-new facility, and so we broke ground on a $14 million complex of buildings and parking lots in a part of town called Canyon View. We completed it and moved into the place in 2001, and from there, things just got bigger.

And yet, things didn't necessarily get better. From a distance of thirty years, I think back to the early days, and I feel nostalgic for the simplicity of our services and our ministries. I know I look through rose-colored glasses, but I still feel that what we were doing was good, that what we were offering was what people wanted and needed. That was true through so much of the growth.

But at a certain point, we crossed a threshold, and I wondered what had happened to my earlier vision. Somehow, I got lost in the growth, and I didn't realize that the organization was taking on a life of its own, a life that was far beyond what I had imagined at the genesis. I no longer felt like I could steer its direction; instead, it began to steer me.

The simple and basic administration of the organization was overwhelming. Our mortgage payment on the new building was $30,000 a month. We also had fifty-three employees, plus expenses—exorbitant electric bills, and costs for the dozens of different ministries we had on top of that. If we weren't bringing in $300,000 a month in tithes, we couldn't pay the bills. So I talked about money in my sermons often, and we calculated how much each person coming in the door would generate.

At some point, I began delivering messages designed not to ruffle any feathers because I needed everyone to come back the next week. We were spending tons of money on audiovisual effects to keep the congregation interested and entertained, and we were marketing ourselves all over the valley to keep people coming through the doors. Of course, I still wanted to help people, but I got to the point where the foremost worry in my mind was to keep the whole institution going.

In essence, the church became a business, where we worried about keeping our "customers" happy, constantly looking at our "bottom line." Each week, I studied the receipts from each service to see what came in, and that told me how much I needed to bring in the next. With those numbers in mind, I designed a message hoping to blow people away so they would help us meet our obligations. Some Sundays, I'd pull into the parking lot and mutter a small prayer—"Oh, God, I hope we have a good weekend." When the receipts were low, I would rack my brain to try to figure out what I had done wrong.

Within a year of building the new church campus, I would walk through the hallways of this huge, expensive, and—by all objective measures—awesome facility, thinking, *What have I done?*

It was a strange and paradoxical thing. I knew building that church was an enviable accomplishment, and it conferred on me a certain sense of importance. At pastors' conferences, I was no longer the guy who sat at the sidelines, watching the other pastors with their black briefcases, wishing I could fit in so much that I ran to a department store in between sessions to buy a black briefcase like theirs. Instead, people wanted to talk to me. They wanted to find out *my* secrets of success; they wanted to do what *I* had done. It was an ego trip, and the pride that went with it was hard to avoid. Every Sunday morning, I would speak to hundreds of people. Then the auditorium would empty, and hundreds more would show up for the second service. That kind of affirmation kept me going for a long time, even when I was running on fumes. It kept me in the church three years past my limit, kept me there all the way to the breaking point.

So to move back to those moments where I walked through the halls thinking, *What is this?*, thinking, *What have I done?*, I can only answer myself one way: I lost focus. I got caught up in the gravity of the organization, in the glitter of its success, which was my success. Instead of sticking with the core of who I wanted us to be—a church for the unchurched, a place that was informal and flexible and attuned to the needs of the congregation, a place with the love of Jesus at its center—we grew past our peak size, past our most favorable dynamic, and we became indiscernible from other Christian churches.

Sadly, it wasn't until it was too late that I realized I had created a burdensome, unwieldy institution that was unrecognizable as the church I had imagined. It was when I realized this that I knew that I couldn't continue on and be okay.

And all of it made me wonder if this was what Jesus had in mind when he sent his disciples to spread the Good News.

Recently I came across a quotation that encapsulates the paradox I wrestled with for years: that Christianity is Jesus' *intuition* but Paul's *institution*.

Even in a cursory reflection on the New Testament, I can see this is true. Jesus went around touching lives, issuing a radical message of love, compassion, forgiveness; telling of a new covenant from God that would extend to Gentiles as well as Jews, to the rich and the poor, to the sick and the well, to men and women. He drew crowds of thousands, but he never built a church building or established a seat of church governance. The only time I see him organizing people was when he fed the five thousand, and he had his disciples break them down into smaller groups so the food could be distributed among them.

No, Jesus was no administrator; he was much closer to the Holy Spirit in John, chapter 3: "The wind blows wherever it pleases. You hear its sound, but you cannot tell where it comes from or where it is going. So it is with everyone born of the Spirit."

Instead, it was Paul who took on the mantle of building an institution, undertaking the job of spreading the Good News with more fervor than even the Twelve. He traveled all over the ancient world planting churches, and yet his letters reveal a striking truth: that almost as soon as he won converts, he was in the business of administration. He was writing back prescriptions about what behavior was acceptable and what was not. He was writing back as an arbiter, advising people how to settle their disputes and organize themselves. He was writing back exhorting people to stick with it, to continue to have faith, to stay in line.

I do not mean to undermine Paul by pointing this out. I admire his fervor and his faith and the pivotal role he played in spreading the gospel. But I do think it's important to keep in mind that organizations, while they can be immensely powerful, often take on a life of their own. The hard way, I learned that institutions are inherently bureaucratic and impersonal. At a certain point, they begin to establish their own gravity, and everything else gets pulled into the orbit of that body.

Most organizations start like my tiny church, with a few people banding together for a common cause. Some of these groups fail, while others blossom into institutions that society as a whole benefits from. Hospitals named after some great saint or groups like the Salvation Army are founded out of compassion for humanity, and many of these groups do incredible work. They put in practices that make them efficient and keep them focused on their original mission. And honestly, the fact that they are large, long-standing, credible, and recognizable institutions is what allows them to accomplish the amount of good they do.

The rise of megachurches was a phenomenon that looked to channel the potential of these large institutions—they sought to become centers where people could come and seek God, even anonymously if they wanted to, on any day of the week; and to offer any ministry that a person could ever want, to be a smorgasbord for believers to choose from. One of the benefits was that diversity—you can come to Wednesday night, Sunday morning, or Saturday night; you can put your child in this group or that one; you can go to either the contemporary or the traditional worship service.

Unsurprisingly, many of the most successful churches are modeled much like corporations to accomplish these great goals. I once read a study that showed that of the most successful pastors—the ones with the largest churches and the biggest budgets—80 percent of them came out of the business world, and only 20 percent came out of seminaries and Bible colleges.

Undoubtedly, this model was successful. (At least for a while; new statistics show these megachurches, which were thriving in the 1990s, began following the mainline churches into decline in the 2000s.) But with the gain in numbers and all the trappings that go with it, there are definite costs.

One is that the bureaucracy grows. I can't tell you how many hours I spent in meetings with employees at every level of the church, not discussing the Bible or the journey of life or the Christian walk, but working out snags in the machine. As the organization grew, the list of problems only seemed to grow larger continually, and as the senior pastor, I felt I had to provide all the answers, all the time. It was an exhausting prospect.

And managing all these different people, people whose needs were in conflict with one another and who thought their area of the church was the most important, was unbelievably difficult and tense. I can remember certain meetings where I felt as though it would have been most appropriate for me to wear a referee shirt and a whistle. Somehow I had believed that by hiring Christians to run the church, we would be set apart and "better than"; we'd be able to deal with our problems as a paradigm of Christian kindness and gentleness. But we bickered and fought, we were petty and unkind, just like any other organization or business. We were all broken, and as much as we tried to hide it, our brokenness broke through the walls of pretense.

I watched this for many years, and I imagined that one day, just over the horizon, we would be past the bureaucratic challenges and settle into the heart of the work. I thought we would hit a plateau where the organization would run smoothly, where everyone would be content, where policies and procedures would all be in place and, like a well-oiled machine, the organization would conduct its business. But until the day I left, Canyon View Vineyard was mired in tiresome bureaucracy that distracted us from the core of our mission.

And this leads to a second problem with organizations—that they can become incredibly inefficient, and the bigger they get, the more resources they have to use inefficiently. One example of our inefficiency was an event we did every Fourth of July, something we called servant evangelism. Modeled on a project started by a pastor friend of mine in Cincinnati, we took part in a citywide Fourth of July celebration at a local park. There we had events for people of every age. We had bands play, we had face-painting booths for the kids, and we provided free food and drinks. Thousands of people would show up and take part during the day, and they'd stay for the fireworks that commenced when the sun set and the sky went dark.

Undoubtedly, it was an amazing project every year. But the cost was significant, both in terms of the two hundred volunteers who were needed to staff this all-day event and the financial cost, as well as in the headache of getting the correct permits from the city for our activities. We did it year after year, but if I'm honest, I don't know how much headway we made with our primary purpose, which was to evangelize, to bring people to Jesus (and to our church). Instead of spending so many of our resources in this inefficient, taxing way, why didn't we just equip people to be in the community, to live their lives showing the light of Christ? Why didn't we advise them to bring a cooler of drinks and some hot dogs, spread a blanket on the ground, and talk to their neighbors?

This wasn't the only event we did that required such energy and resources. Twice a year, we had to have ministry fairs, where whole weekend services were dedicated to recruiting volunteers for each of our ministries. There were times I didn't want to walk down the halls of the administration office complex because I knew there were going to be requests for things to help cope with the growing demands of the organization—requests for new equipment, for more volunteers, for more time. The needs seemed never-ending.

And really, the different ministries were each like the organization itself—there seemed to be a demand that they perpetuate themselves. Each ministry and event became set in stone and had to be replicated year in and year out, seemingly in bigger and better fashion. As I watched this, I wondered about this compulsive need we had to institutionalize every activity, that things could never be spontaneous and in the moment.

A great example of this was something that happened outside the church with a close friend of mine named Ruthie. Several years ago, she was out one night having drinks with some friends, and one of the ladies suggested that they buy each other gifts for Christmas. Ruthie, who can be very blunt, said, "I don't need anything, and quite honestly, I don't *want* to buy you anything."

Because of her honesty, the ladies were able to admit they didn't need anything either, so instead, they decided to help a few families who were struggling to buy Christmas gifts for their children. Through some local churches and charities, they found about nine families who needed help, and they went out and bought presents and delivered them to the families.

It was a great success, and the next year, other people found out about it and joined in. The number of families served jumped up from nine to fifty-four. Though Ruthie was excited that these families were benefiting, she decided that making this a yearly commitment was not what she wanted to do. She had chosen to do something because she felt moved, and it was spontaneous. She had never meant to fetter herself to a yearly responsibility; some acts can be organic acts of kindness. It was not her burden to carry every year, but a good example that people could take and pay forward.

In many ways, I wished that our church could have been more like Ruthie—more sensitive to the needs at the moment, serving spontaneously and fully, but without some burdensome organization to complicate things. At a certain point, it seemed like all of the flexibility of the organization was gone, and it felt like we could never just be moved by the spirit to serve a certain family, to help out with an emergent need.

And this leads into a third problem with organizations: they become inflexible. Given that resources are limited, both financially and in human labor, there is only a certain amount that we as a church—or any organization for that matter—could accomplish. Even larger foundations know their focus must be narrowed, or they become a river a mile wide and an inch deep. We knew that even in a small town like Grand Junction, even with a large church like ours, we could stretch ourselves to the breaking point, and still there would be many needs untouched.

So as time passed, we developed policies to narrow our focus and to protect ourselves from being overburdened by demands from local nonprofits and charities as well as individuals. One policy was that if people came and asked for money, we'd give them prepaid cards they could use for gas at a local gas station. But it was heartbreaking to have to deny people the help they needed. It was distressing that, after labeling ourselves as a compassionate, caring followers of Christ, we often had to turn people away, even people who were members in our church. I understood the policies—often I had a hand in putting them in place—but I was still unsettled when we couldn't pay someone's electric bill, or when someone came to us with a worthwhile charity in desperate need of support and we had to say no. Sometimes, I just wanted to help them myself, but I knew my own resources and energies were finite and couldn't extend to every person in need in our community either.

Of course, organizations always have their limits. Even Jesus could only do so much, and when he left this planet, there were still plenty of needs he didn't meet. Yet our policies did not come from Mount Sinai, and if I had it to do over again, I would place the individual first, instead of steamrolling the person with the strict, inflexible policies we put in place to protect the organization.

Lately I have been really taken by the idea of certain movements, or what we would call in the evangelical world "moves of God," being of a generation. One example might be the Jesus People movement of the late '60s and early '70s in Southern California, where thousands of hippies had true conversion experiences that led them to Jesus Christ. This new wave brought cataclysmic changes to Protestant churches, transforming many of them into places where people could dress and speak and act informally.

The same thing happened with the rise of the megachurches, many of which were founded in the wake of this shift. But there are rumblings of decline in the evangelical world. A whole generation has passed, and as with every generation, many of the leaders see the challenges in front of them—how society has changed again, how their numbers are falling, how young people are no longer joining up like they did twenty years ago. As Diana Butler Bass points out, "Young adults are far more likely to be [religiously unaffiliated] than their more religiously obligated grandparents—somewhere between 25 and 30 percent of adults under thirty claim no religious affiliation."[9]

Many conservative voices in the church are lamenting this trend. Many are wondering how to pull the young back in. Many are repeating the question that people have been asking since that movement began: "How can we keep it alive and fresh?"

I know; I was one of those voices for many years.

But since my disillusionment, I'm not so afraid of change, nor am I so sure that the way we have always done things needs to be the way we do things in the future. Not every movement is meant to continue in perpetuity, and this might just be a movement away from such large, impersonal, corporate organizations toward a different type of faith. As Bass explains, "Some things will cease to work, no longer make sense, and fail to give comfort or provide guidance...Religions lose their power to inspire. But that only means we have work to do here and now—to find new paths of meaning, new ways to connect with God, to form new communities, and to organize ways of making the world a better place."[10]

Maybe she is right; maybe we need to think outside of the current models for a new step on this spiritual path. In Acts, it says that David served his generation, and then he slept with his fathers. For me, that was a profound insight, a biblical precedent for me to serve my generation and rest, and even for a movement to serve its generation and then rest. David's retirement, my own retirement, and maybe the end of these churches as we know them might be what Dr. Henry Cloud calls "necessary endings": things that have to end for something new to have life.

And in my mind, leaving behind the megachurch might not be a bad thing, given its unwieldiness and the toll it takes on the people who lead it. For me, it was a tremendous burden, but it wasn't until just before I quit that I understood why. In the months before I resigned as pastor, I began seeing a counselor to try to make sense of all of the things that were going wrong in my life, the things that weren't getting better despite all of my fervent prayer. And at one point she said very simply, "The church owns you." The words emerging from her lips hit my heart with such impact, I felt as though someone had punched me. I've never had a statement transfix me the way that one did.

I began thinking of the ways it was true. I thought about my fear that people were keeping track of how many hours I spent at the church. I thought about the way I felt beholden to be there every Sunday because if I took a weekend off and one of our junior pastors was speaking, our attendance would go down. It was impossible to be there all the time, but at a conference one year, I heard a man explain how, to succeed, a pastor had to be there forty-five weeks out of the year. And I just remember feeling overwhelmed by the responsibility to keep the church going administratively, but also to inspire thousands of people every Sunday for forty-five weeks out of the year—so inspired that they would come back every week and tithe so we could keep things going.

And then I thought about how I could never find rest—how I tried to reserve Mondays as my day off, how Cheryl and I would promise ourselves we weren't going to answer the phone, only to find ourselves picking it up when it rang. The first statement out of the person's mouth would be, "I know this is your day off, but . . ." Even if we just went grocery shopping here in Grand Junction, people would see us and bring up different issues about the church—about finances, about another program, another meeting, and all I could think about was the church, almost every minute of every day.

I thought about how I had no hobbies and no friends outside of church. At a conference at Willow Creek, Bill Hybels asked us what we did for fun, and I had no answer. Another time, an acquaintance asked the same thing—"What do you do for entertainment?" I couldn't answer. All I did was church.

I thought of how one Sunday, I watched a woman approach me after the service, and I knew what she wanted. She was going to write a book, and she wanted me to read the manuscript. As she was walking up to me, in my mind, I was saying, *I am going to say no to her.* But when she asked me, you know what came out of my mouth? I said, "Sure." I was so afraid of making anyone feel dismissed or rejected that I couldn't even live a life of my own.

It seemed like even with all of the people we hired to help, even with the team of pastors we brought on to spread out the responsibility, there was never enough of me to go around. Even standing out in the lobby before a service to shake people's hands became a problem, because people want to talk to their pastor, so they stop and begin pouring out their lives, but you've got a service to conduct, and another after that, and it just becomes a rock too big to push up the hill. From living it, I can see why pastors become isolated. The demands are so absolutely draining in every way—emotionally, mentally, physically, and spiritually—that you feel like your only choice is to isolate yourself from the crowds to keep your head above water.

Other pastors feel it too. I saw a survey one time that said 70 percent of pastors would quit their jobs if they could find another with equal pay and security. Only recently, a pastor's wife called me and explained that her husband was burned out and done, but he couldn't get out of the ministry because he couldn't find anything else to do. For me, it was definitely a challenge to figure out what to do next—what could I possibly do after having reigned over my tiny kingdom?

So when this counselor told me that the church owned me, I knew she was absolutely right in so many ways, and that she had given words to something I had known intuitively for a long time. I knew that all of my time and effort went into the church, and far less attention was given to my own needs and the needs of my family. Even worse, I knew that I was imprisoned by an image, the image that my church wanted from me, the image of a man who was endlessly giving, endlessly available, endlessly patient, someone who had everything worked out and did everything right.

In their eyes, I was a super-Christian superman on a pedestal.

This was not only true for me. It's true for virtually every pastor. Pastors are expected to life perfect lives, and they're supposed to have perfect families. Having been on the other side of it, I know pastors' lives are not perfect. My childhood pastor's life was a mess. My friends who are pastors have messy lives. And mine was obviously a disaster.

But we don't share that brokenness, and I think that's partly because a church doesn't want an imperfect pastor. How can you inspire and be transparent at the same time? How can you be a spiritual guide as well as a real person? Our congregations deny that we are broken, vulnerable humans, and when they see that we have feet of clay, they are devastated.

Living with that responsibility was a burden, and at a certain point, I cracked under its weight. I can remember a moment when I was speaking, and the thought flashed through my mind, *How can you be telling them to live this way when you can't do it yourself? How do you advise them on how to live their lives when yours is coming unraveled?* It floored me, and I stopped in midsentence. Maybe ten seconds—ten slow, painful seconds—passed before I regained my composure enough to go on.

On a sabbatical I took right after my breakdown, I read a book called *Leaving Church*, by Barbara Brown Taylor. Taylor had been the pastor of a small Episcopalian church in rural Georgia. It was a life she thought she wanted—the perfect church building with the perfect-sized congregation, living in the perfect house on the perfect piece of land. Only five years in, she too buckled under the weight of the demands of the office and resigned.

But she stayed in the small town, and soon after, she was invited to a birthday party. As the night wore on and people got a little tipsy, they started throwing one another into the pool. And as they came up to grab her, they suddenly stopped and said, "Oh, no. We can't do that to you." It broke her heart. She was thinking, *But I'm exactly like you.*

That really captured my feeling—that I just wanted to be like everyone else. I wanted to be seen for who I was, not for the person people expected me to be. I wanted to be Dan, not some figure on a pedestal. I wanted to break down the wall that separated me from everyone else, the wall that was established by the simple word *pastor* in front of my name.

It happened all the time, both at church and in the community. Back when I did weddings, I'd perform the marriage ceremony, and I'd have everyone's respect because I was officiating. Then I'd go to the reception, where there was alcohol and dancing and all the rest, and I'd feel like a pork chop in a synagogue. I was so out of place. I think that's one of the reasons why Jesus said don't call anybody "Father"—because it puts up these boundaries. And Jesus didn't abide the traditional hierarchies. His kingdom is exactly upside down.

For me, that's been a true revelation. It was a revelation to realize that the elevation of the pastor as this mythic figure is just that—a myth. It's also been a revelation to me that my "calling" to be a pastor was no more a calling than the life work of anybody else who is meeting a need. One of my colleagues at hospice is a social worker who is one of the most gifted people I have ever been around in my life. She is incredibly intelligent, and she has an amazing way of getting people to share the exact information she needs so that she can apply the correct resources. It's absolutely phenomenal to watch. We give an award called the Heart of Hospice, and she would win it every year if they didn't require different people to be nominated. That's a true calling.

What I see now is that people have incredible gifts. If you go and observe nurses and certified nursing assistants (CNAs) at hospice, you see people not only using their gifts, but also meeting a need and manifesting incredible compassion. I watch those nurses and those CNAs, and the way they serve these people who are suffering is unbelievable. Some of the deepest, most meaningful conversations are the ones that occur between a hospice patient and a CNA. I think these people are truly answering a calling, and they are truly serving others and washing people's feet.

In the eyes of the church, that's not what appears to matter. What matters is the number of people you get to come to church on Sunday, or the number you "saved" during your altar call.

But if we look at Jesus, when the big crowds came around, he usually left. Instead of crowds, he was after that personal touch. He was finding the one guy at the pool of Bethesda who had lain there for thirty-eight years. I understand how it has become so prevalent for churches to measure their success in quantitative terms, because success is measured by numbers in most parts of our lives. But with Jesus, it was about the individual touches.

For me, the entire definition of *ministry* has changed. Ministry for me isn't just about salvation. In this world where we are lonely, confused, and heartbroken, where we are struggling to find work and put food on the table for tomorrow, ministry is not about perpetuating an institution or abiding by the rules and regulations of an organization.

Instead, ministry is meeting a need.

Jesus always connected ministry with need. They were hungry, he fed them. They were blind, he gave them sight. They were discouraged, he encouraged them. They were dead, he raised them.

I believe that when we think about the way to move forward, that should be a central, unswerving goal and focus: how do we meet needs?

Only a few days ago, I met a young man at the hospice center who is studying to become a nurse through the local college here in Grand Junction. He had gone to Canyon View Vineyard several years ago, and he said to me, "You don't remember me, but you changed my life." Through tears, he explained that his life had been in shambles when he started coming, and we helped him turn himself around. That's one of those things I hear that still touches me. That's one of those moments that makes me feel that maybe my work was worthwhile, despite the difficulties.

But I don't miss it. It was a tremendous ego boost, but the downside was what it cost me. The expectations were too high, and the demands were too many.

The conclusion that I am coming to is that I'm not sure a person can start a church, nurture it to a place with a huge following, and still have a family and be vibrant.

And I don't know that, in the long term, a church like that really nurtures people into their full spiritual potential. I don't know that it encourages people to continue moving forward. When I was working to keep Canyon View Vineyard going, I was not first and foremost concerned with the spiritual maturity of my congregation. In fact, it was better for me if they didn't grow up, if they didn't mature, because that meant they would continue to be dependent on me for sustenance. They'd have to keep coming back to Canyon View, and I could keep the institution going. I am not proud of this, and I don't think I did it consciously, but looking back, I can see that keeping them at the status quo was better because it meant that I could count on them to keep the church alive. I've almost come to the point where I think we've screwed it all up—that this way of doing church, having them come back to the same old thing week after week, is not a way to have true communion with one another and with God. I think that there are probably better, simpler ways of achieving this connection.

Here's what I mean: For about a year after I resigned, I imposed a type of exile on myself. I left town, and I kept myself out of the public eye in every way I could.

Instead, I spent a lot of time with people around a table of good food and drinks. Some were believers, and we would share our ideas about God and life, and for weeks afterward, I could feast on the riches of those conversations. They lifted me more than any revival, more than any Sunday service. I was finding the ideas we were sharing new and invigorating, and they helped me feel closer to God, a true feat during that desperate time. Where before I had felt only despair, I began to see flickers of new life.

And yet, these gatherings were simple and spontaneous, and I began to wonder if this wasn't the kind of fellowship Jesus was wanting his followers to enjoy—a fellowship much like he experienced while here on the earth; an authentic, deep connection with others seeking to make meaning out of life, seeking to live the compassionate message of Christ.

I'm not suggesting we do away with the church as we know it, but I believe there is a time for people to reflect on where they are in their spiritual pilgrimage. For me, there was a time to leave church. I haven't been for several years now, and though I miss some of the people I knew there, I don't miss the judgment, the pressure to conform, the feeling that everyone is watching. I think many others feel the same way I do, as each year, more and more people abandon organized religion.

Which leads us to the big question, one that has weighed on my mind for years and one that is being turned over in the heads of every person who has left behind the safe harbor of traditional Christianity and is now somewhat aimlessly floating out to sea: where do we go from here?

And my answer is, very simply, *onward.*

CHAPTER 12

ONWARD, FOR AN UNRIGHTEOUS STEWARD

And Jesus told his disciples:

> There was a rich man whose manager was accused of wasting his possessions. So he called him in and asked him, "What is this I hear about you? Give an account of your management, because you cannot be manager any longer."
>
> The manager said to himself, "What shall I do now? My master is taking away my job. I'm not strong enough to dig, and I'm ashamed to beg—I know what I'll do so that, when I lose my job here, people will welcome me into their houses."
>
> So he called in each one of his master's debtors. He asked the first, "How much do you owe my master?"
>
> "Nine hundred gallons of olive oil," he replied.
>
> The manager told him, "Take your bill, sit down quickly, and make it four hundred and fifty."
>
> Then he asked the second, "And how much do you owe?"
>
> "A thousand bushels of wheat," he replied.
>
> He told him, "Take your bill and make it eight hundred."
>
> The master commended the dishonest manager because he had acted shrewdly. (Luke 16:1–8)

In the year after I resigned from Canyon View Vineyard, I read this passage on an airplane. Or I should say, I reread it, because over the years, I have come across this parable time and time again, only to be baffled each time. There were

had spoken on it to my congregations, presenting it in the best way I
, at even then, I knew I'd never really gotten it.

At the time I came across the parable on the airplane, I was in a steep downward slide. I had moved out of my house with Cheryl, and we were in the process
of divorcing. I had left town completely and was living about sixty miles from
Grand Junction. Without a job, without the label of pastor to boost my stature
or the successes of the church to make easy conversation, I felt completely lost.
I felt like a failure, and like all of the good things I had done in my life had been
erased by my infidelity. Truthfully, part of me wanted to wallow for a little while,
to sink down in self-pity and utter exhaustion and languish there. Somewhere I
knew that my recent failure wasn't my whole life, but failure was the only thing
I could really feel at that time. I was in a tailspin.

So when I read the parable of the unrighteous steward that day on the airplane, my paradigm had shifted enough that I could finally identify with him, as
I had with John the Baptist just after my breakdown. My place in the world had
changed enough that I could see through the unrighteous steward's eyes.

What I learned is a simple lesson. It isn't rooted in the historical or cultural
context in which Jesus lived, and it doesn't depend on a rigorous translation of
Greek or Aramaic or Hebrew. It is that Jesus commended the unrighteous steward
because he refused to wallow in his mistakes; instead, he immediately began to
do what he could to salvage his life.

The steward goes to his master's debtors, and he nurtures his relationships
with them by cutting their debts down. As some biblical scholars read this, he is
cutting out his own portion of the money in order to build new relationships that
will help him move forward in his life.

When the unrighteous steward asks, "What shall I do now?" it seems so simple, and he acts so quickly that it seems like cutting down the debts was an easy
thing to do. But in my own life, it wasn't a question with an easy answer. When
I asked it of myself, I was at a complete loss. Should I relocate to a town where
my past wouldn't find me? Should I hide in anonymity and begin anew? Or
should I return to Grand Junction and face the town and its judgment? Should I
go back and find a different job and refuse to let my mistakes define who I was?

For months, I couldn't decide. I knew for certain that I couldn't go back to
the ministry, but being a pastor was so much of my identity that a new path was
not immediately apparent.

So I stayed in that small town for half a year, as days and weeks and months passed, and I began writing, pouring all of my questions and frustration and heartbreak with God into a manuscript that would grow and evolve into this book. I spent hours on the Internet looking for resources to help me understand what I was going through, and I learned that what I was going through wasn't uncommon—that preachers are one of the two professions most likely to experience burnout. I learned why I had burned out in the first place: I had never set boundaries. So during those long months, I taught myself to say *No*. In essence, I spent that year learning how to take care of myself.

To this day, this is a huge problem in contemporary evangelical circles—that there is actually no teaching, no modeling about how to care for yourself. In fact, self-care isn't ever mentioned, because if you are taking time for yourself, you aren't giving yourself; you are being selfish. But I had given of myself to the point that there was almost nothing left to give, and I had to do something to pull all of my pieces back together.

Eventually, as I cared for myself and gained perspective on my life and my loss, I realized that I couldn't continue dwelling on my transgression; I couldn't allow it to overwhelm me. I needed to remake my life, but I couldn't do that looking in the rearview mirror.

Unrighteous steward though I was, I had to move forward, to go onward. After losing my family, my career, and my faith, I had to answer the question, *What will I do now?*

In August of 2008, I began moving forward. I returned to Grand Junction. My mother had fallen ill to the point that we thought she wasn't going to make it, so I came back to take part in her care. By then, I had recuperated enough to begin looking for a new job. I heard about an opening for a chaplain at the hospice center where my mother had gone for care, so I applied and got it.

My job is not an easy job. In visiting families and patients to counsel them on death and loss, I bear witness to a lot of struggle and pain. But I have also learned so much, and my time with hospice has played an important role in shaping my understanding of life and loss, which has complemented and reinforced my understanding of the unrighteous steward.

There is nothing like the specter of death to bring life, faith, and loss into intense focus. At hospice, I have learned that the best way to deal with loss is by fully facing it, head-on, with full honesty and acceptance. What clients have taught me is a huge lesson in reality—that we cannot deny our losses. I lost my family. I lost my career. I lost my marriage. I *lost*. And they are teaching me that it's okay, that this was a part of my path, and that there's something redemptive about going through the grieving process. My disillusionment and my crisis of faith are not the end. There will be life afterward, and I have faith that it will be a better one.

The new concept I have of God makes room for this reading of the unrighteous steward. I don't think God is in heaven keeping account of every mistake I have made in order to hold it against me, because if I believed that, then I couldn't move forward. I'd be trapped by that focus on my mistakes, which are great indeed, and in some ways, unforgivable.

No, I think that our loving, forgiving, merciful God looks down on us with hope; that even when we stumble, we will get back up. People who have been raised in the church live with this tension that if we don't do it right, then we are out, sometimes to the point that it feels like a tightrope walk across the Grand Canyon, with no room for error.

But God has wide, wide latitude, and he has a lot of mercy.

So you get it wrong. Big deal. It's what you do afterward. In Proverbs it says, "For though a righteous man falls seven times, he rises again."

And that's the parable of the unrighteous steward. It's what you do afterward. It's not that you were disillusioned. It's what you do afterward. It's not the end when you have lost your faith. There is life after that. Being disillusioned is just the beginning. You just have to move onward on the journey to build a more authentic faith for yourself.

Truly, that possibility is incredibly exciting. When I realized that I could rebuild my life and my faith, that there was a chance to start something new, to make my own life that wasn't shaped by the rules and regulations of an institution but that could emerge from my own conscience and my own life experiences, I was elated.

When I began moving on, I had the sense that what I was doing was right and that something better was coming in my life. Despite the fact that I had lost my familiar life, despite the fact that I'd lost my career, I knew I was going to be me again. I realized that what I had lost over all those years I was going to regain, that I would be comfortable in my own skin. I wasn't going to be what the church had made me or what my dysfunctional marriage had made me. I had lost myself, but I began a journey to gain my life back.

Almost ten years ago, paramedics rushed a man to a hospital in Grand Junction with a traumatic injury. News crews were all over the story of Aaron Ralston, who had gone hiking by himself in Canyonlands National Park in Utah, just a few hours west of here. In a slot canyon, a boulder fell and pinned Ralston's forearm against the wall of the canyon. For five days, he waited and slowly sipped water from his canteen, trying to ration it as long as possible. When he ran out, he carved his name, his birth date, and his presumed death date on the sandstone walls and videotaped a good-bye message to his family.

Yet he didn't die that night, and when he awoke on the sixth day, he had somehow rediscovered the will to live. As gruesomely chronicled in the movie *127 Hours,* Ralston amputated his own arm below the elbow, then began an arduous hike back to his car, a hike that required him to rappel a sixty-five-foot wall with his one hand and an eight-mile trek in the blazing midday sun.

Luckily, he encountered a Dutch family who tended to him while they called for help. Search helicopters had already been sent out for him (his parents had reported him missing, and they had narrowed the search to the Canyonlands), and they soon found him and rushed him to surgery in Grand Junction, where he was stabilized and began recovering.

In May of 2007, four years after his accident, Ralston gave a speech at the Swiss Economic Forum. In it, he acknowledged that he had lost his hand, but in return he had gained his life. Ralston's story is incredible, full of determination and grit and strength that I can't imagine. But as with many great lessons, Ralston's words really moved me to think about my own life. I had lost my past—my marriage, my career, my status in the community—in order to gain my own life.

Of course, my journey was figurative in comparison to Ralston's. But over the course of decades, I had become trapped. I had abdicated all of my own thinking and decision making to an impersonal institution. I had deferred to what others thought I should do instead of developing my own moral compass. And I had believed against all evidence to the contrary that God would always save me from suffering, and that if I just prayed hard enough, he'd take care of all the tough decisions.

It wasn't until that feeling of being trapped was so overwhelming, so much so that I considered ending my own life, that I took drastic measures to get myself out. It's often true that crisis precipitates change. To keep my life, I had to cut ties with those things that were keeping me from moving onward, personally and spiritually. I had to say good-bye to my old ways of thinking, my old faith practices, and my familiar habits. To again use the term from Dr. Henry Cloud, these were "necessary endings," like pruning a tree so that it can flourish and grow.

These changes weren't easy to make. But at a certain point, you reach a threshold where you can't maintain the status quo anymore. As Anais Nin once said, "And the day came when the risk to remain tight in a bud was more painful than the risk it took to blossom."

In my life now, I have blossomed. I believe I have grown into a spiritually mature and contented person. I have retrieved some parts of my character I thought were long gone, like the lightheartedness that had disappeared under the weight of my old life. With friends and family, I feel so much more relaxed now that I am not trying to live according to some perfect Christian standard, and I find that I have more open, transparent relationships.

Instead of some model, I am just a fellow sojourner in life, and it's nice to have people look at me that way instead of as the authority figure with all the answers. I can sit and share a couple beers with people. I can let people speak their minds, what's on their hearts. I can have great conversations with the liberal social workers at hospice, conversations that are real efforts at understanding each other, not correcting or converting each other. I can share my more conservative leanings, and we can walk away with no hard feelings. There is so much flexibility and so much latitude and so much freedom that I find myself smiling when I think about it.

On top of this, I am probably in the most comfortable place I have ever been with God. I don't wake up each day with heaviness about why he is not acting in my life. I am not searching every day for a little sign from him or questioning what I've done wrong, why he's ignoring me, his most faithful servant. I don't expect huge things of him—in fact, I don't expect much of him at all. I'm taking a lot more responsibility for my life, and I feel better about making those decisions, not blaming God. If I do something right, I can feel good that I did it. I'm just trying to experience good things, to live with loving-kindness, and to meet him where I can.

In the movie *Chariots of Fire,* the missionary Eric Liddell says that when he ran, he felt like God was smiling on him because he was using his talents in the way he was created. I used to feel like that when I was speaking about God from my heart, often from the pulpit, but at a certain point, that didn't happen anymore. Instead, I felt an absence, even though I was busy doing what I thought was God's work. Christianity teaches that the most important thing is to be connected with God, yet somehow we get caught up in this process of *doing*. But *doing* is not the goal—the goal is *being*. The story of Martha and Mary is the perfect example. Mary sat at Jesus's feet while Martha bustled about, compulsively *doing* for Jesus. When Martha got upset that Mary wasn't helping, she pleaded with him to get Mary to help. Always the one to surprise, Jesus chastised Martha. He told her that Mary had picked the better part.

It's taken me decades to learn this lesson, but I finally get it, and now I can feel God's presence when I am just *being*. A couple of years ago, I drove my motorcycle up to Grand Mesa, the big, flat-topped mountain that overlooks Grand Junction, with a nice lunch and a couple of beers and my fishing pole. I caught two fish and turned them both back. And after a few hours, I decided to head home. When I was coming off the mountain on my bike, all of a sudden there was a presence—a peace, a calm—that almost sent shivers up and down my spine. I knew then I hadn't felt that fulfilled in years. I was humbled, wondering after all my wanderings why I deserved such a euphoric encounter with the Divine.

It's as simple as this: I didn't earn it. I didn't work for it. It wasn't because I snapped my fingers or said "in Jesus' name." There was solace to feel that God was outside of that structure.

God shows up when he wants to, and he's very, very gracious when he does.

This new, authentic faith life I live is so different from any form of faith I ever thought I'd practice. I thought it would always be in a church with a worship song that I'd feel close to God, or it'd be during my quiet time as I read Scripture and prayed. But at a certain point, I realized those things didn't feed me, and I am only sad that it took me so long to find that God could meet me in new ways.

As I have said before, I can't go to church anymore, at least not right now. I'm pretty sure my mother attends each prayer meeting with a heart full of worry for her wayward son, but I just can't force myself through the doors. It just doesn't make sense for my life anymore.

Still I long for a faith community, but the one I imagine is much different from what I spent my life building. If I started a new "church," we wouldn't have a building or regular, scheduled services. Instead, I would follow the model of

Jesus, surrounding myself with a small core of friends, with people with no other agenda than to walk together in this journey to find God. My vision of church would be full of replenishing relationships, not an obligation that takes more and more effort to participate in as the years go by.

If we look at what Jesus did, he didn't schedule a weekly meeting with people in an expensive new building. He went out among them, and he taught them the way. They'd go out and try to practice what he taught, and if they didn't get it right, they'd come back and say, "Hey, we need some help." Mostly, they were experiencing life together. I think that church as relationship and as community is the form that teaches us how to love one another—when we go through similar experiences together and we can talk openly about them.

My hope for people who are seeking God would be that they'd come from all walks of life to share their journey, with no ulterior motive to change or convert people. The main goal would be to love one another and to work on the relationships that Jesus encouraged when he said, "I will know that you are my disciples if you have love one for another."

And as with Christ and his Twelve, I'd want it to be small enough that the group could retain its flexibility and its humanness. As the early church grew, Paul was always writing back to straighten out the structure and mitigate some crisis. Jesus didn't have that problem. He had these smaller groups that needed less structure and fewer rules, and had greater flexibility. So the numbers don't matter—it's the quality of relationships that a group can produce, and the flexibility to grow and change as people move along the path.

In my vision of a new church, maybe there would be a leader, but maybe it would just be a community, where everybody worked together in humility and compassion. If we look at Christ, he led; but when his disciples asked who would sit at his right and left hands, Jesus pulled a child out of the crowd and said, "You have to become like one of these to enter my kingdom." He taught that following him was serving, not being served, not being at the top of the totem pole. In effect, Jesus reversed all the religious hierarchy. He said, "If you want to be great in the kingdom of God, you must humble yourself." And he washed their feet.

In my own experience, the hierarchy of the church precludes that type of intimacy, that type of commitment, that type of service. Instead, the distance between the pastor and the people gets larger, and the programs are less and less personalized. This is a common feature of growing churches: they become more like corporations, where one size must fit all. The bureaucracy grows in order to

manage the growing numbers, and instead of individual expressions or prefer-
ences, it comes down to Roberts Rules of Order. Yet at that point, the church can't
function how Jesus did, where he stepped in, discovered someone's heart, and
really spoke to that individual's needs.

Larger organizations look to continue their upward climb, and to do that,
they begin looking for shortcuts from other successful leaders. As Diana Butler
Bass points out in *Christianity After Religion,* many churches purchase Vacation
Bible School programs instead of designing their own; or as I did many times,
pastors attend conferences looking for the newest, latest, greatest trend that will
attract more people to the church doors. "Yet spiritual commercialization creates
a culture of sameness across the country that subsumes local cultures in its wake,
losing the quality of neighborly faith," Bass writes.[11] The freshness, the authen-
ticity, and the spontaneity of a particular group are lost. Churches become like
cookie cutters, asking everyone to be the same shape. Orthodoxy takes over, doctrinal statements come to the forefront, and organizational flowcharts become the
subject of meetings.

I know some will try to argue this point and say that Jesus spoke to thousands. And I know that he did, and that in the book of Acts, people met at
Solomon's Portico, a huge plaza near the temple, and the crowds were overwhelming. In fact, Peter spoke there on Pentecost, and over three thousand people
showed up.

So yes, it's true that the numbers were huge. But it also says that afterward,
they went from house to house meeting with people. People still needed individual attention.

I am not proposing that large churches be done away with. A megachurch is
a powerful place for seekers who want to come in and retain their anonymity.
They can come and go and nobody has to know them, and maybe for their spiritual pilgrimage, that works. But it leaves something to be desired in the personal
realm, in the real of relationships, and it doesn't accommodate unconventional
paths. And as I have argued, there's a danger that serving the individual can
become less important than perpetuating the organization.

The message of Christ is not about growing an organization. It's not an agenda
of getting people into church, and by extension, into heaven. As Diana Butler Bass
points out, the word *salvation* comes from the Latin word *salvus,* which means
whole, sound, healed, and safe.[12] To me, this reinforces the idea that our faith journey is about making the world a better place, where people are reconciled to one

another, where healing and wholeness are the goals, not conversion by means of the sinner's prayer. Like mine did, most churches count the number of people attending each service and responding to altar calls because measuring how people are maturing is nearly impossible. But really, we should be helping people become more aware of whether or not there is a sense of wholeness developing inside them.

I think that such communities are possible, communities where we challenge one another, encourage one another, and inspire one another toward good deeds. In isolation, there is no one there to give you resistance, but as the proverb says, "As iron sharpens iron, so one man's countenance sharpens the countenance of another." When someone comes in with a different view of Scripture, it sharpens you. Their reading will either settle what is in your heart, or it will make you work a little harder to reinforce your belief. In Christianity, we've almost given up the idea of reasoning, where we ponder something and research it, and after a while and enough reflection, come to a conclusion.

That's a church I'd want to be a part of now, where people could sit down and articulate their faith. Not mine, but theirs. Just thinking about people being that self-assured, that serious, that well-versed and studied begins to make me smile. I love sitting with people who have questions and are really working toward a conclusion, even if that conclusion may change and deepen later. That is what maturing spiritual people do. They develop their philosophies, their theologies. They wrestle with the ideas, and they write them down. That's what the disciples did. Spiritual people see God in a slightly different light than the person next to them, and they interpret the Bible a little differently, and they respond to the church in a different way.

But we don't give each other the space to do this or the time to work it out. Instead, we think we all have to believe and do exactly the same thing to be a community. But to make everyone believe exactly the same way is not necessarily unity. It can be conformity, but it's not unity.

I believe there can be diversity in unity, and there can be unity in diversity. Once you step away from rigid, narrow pathways that insist there is only one way, you can accept people who have the same goal in seeking God but approach it in different ways. This diversity and opposing ideas would be a great strength. In your arm, you have muscles that are antagonists to one another. Your biceps contract to bend your arm as your triceps elongate. They have to pull and push at the same time to make your arm bend, and the opposite when you straighten it. That's how I feel about how I am living now. The people I break bread with are from different faith backgrounds and live lifestyles that aren't Christian, at least in the traditional sense. But I feel such healing and wholeness that I can be in their presence and I don't have to judge or be angry or worried. And it has humbled me how much they have invited me into their lives. They ask me to come out and have drinks with them; they invite me over to play poker. I feel so connected, like a part of the sea of humanity, and I feel like this journey of reconciliation is what Jesus came to enact on earth.

Jesus came to show "the way," which implies that we are on a journey. In our spiritual lives, we aren't supposed to get comfortable and stagnant, because then we will stop growing. When the children of Israel became stagnant during the Exodus, when they didn't want to move, the cloud carried on, and they had to move with it. That's how I see the Holy Spirit leading us to God.

If a particular path only lasts a little while, there is always the opportunity to do something new. Under the guidance of the Holy Spirit, we go new places; we don't have to continue what we have always done. We can embark on a different pathway that will lead us to the fulfillment that Jesus promised.

The jig is up, as Diana Butler Bass says. People aren't buying the old rules and regulations, the hypocrisy and the judgment, the tired routines of conventional Christianity. Too many times, they've prayed for the miracles their preachers told them would come, and they've been disappointed. Too many times, they have followed the formula, only to find that no formula can force the hand of God. Too many times, they have seen religion in its worst incarnation, rife with judgment and hypocrisy and self-righteousness. Too many times, they've gone to church and found it was irrelevant to their modern lives.

I'm in the same boat. These days, I need a faith that is relevant to the life I live and the freedom to change as I learn and grow. Jesus spoke about not pouring new wine into old wineskins. "No one sews a patch of unshrunk cloth on an old garment, for the patch will pull away from the garment, making the tear worse," Jesus said in the Gospel of Matthew. "Neither do people pour new wine into old wineskins. If they do, the skins will burst; the wine will run out and the wineskins will be ruined. No, they pour new wine into new wineskins, and both are preserved."

Every generation, it seems that someone tries to pour new wine into old wineskins. People insist you have to stick to the way that it was, because you are in the world and not of the world, and you aren't supposed to change with the times. I have gone into churches where it felt as though I was walking through a time warp, where I had just entered the 1950s or 1960s. That's the way it's been, and that's the way it's going to be.

But when you walk in, it's a sea of gray hair.

I'm sure this is something many Christians would decry about the world today—that there is less blind trust in authority, that people deviate from the old beliefs after being exposed to other ideas and philosophies. But we can't change the fact that people have access to information, especially young people raised on science and technology and with all of the world's knowledge at their fingertips.

We can't keep people from seeking, from asking bigger questions, and because of this, the church as we know it, where everyone wears the same harness, where everyone buys into the same belief system, is going to become increasingly difficult to maintain. This is evident in the young people who refuse to leave their individuality and their questions and dissent at the door. The largest proportion of religiously unaffiliated people are under thirty, those who leave home and have a chance to make their own decisions about life and say, "No way. I'm not buying into that." Church leaders can spend a lot of time pointing fingers at factors outside the church—and they do. But in doing that, they refuse to acknowledge that the church is failing to provide the spiritual sustenance that people are hungry for. Instead of getting out in front and providing what people really need, the church is digging its heels in and laying blame on everyone else.

Why is this? Why is the church the tail and not the head? Why do we resist wrestling with the issues of our day in an open debate with our fellow sojourners in this world? Why do we have to refuse new discoveries, new insights, new ideas that could potentially help us get closer to the truth?

Jesus was not afraid of ideas, and he wasn't afraid of change. When he came onto the planet, he engaged with the culture, and he changed what faith looked like. Faith wasn't confined to the synagogues anymore, and it wasn't reserved just for the high priests. Jesus established a way outside of those structures, and it was a way that united people, that reconciled us to one another, and that healed us from our brokenness.

And really, that's what we are hungry for—something to heal us from our brokenness, because we are all broken. Again, it reminds me of the retreat Cheryl and I attended just before we separated, a retreat for pastors and their spouses whose marriages were in crisis, where the leader of the group began the first session with those words: "I feel the safest among broken people."

Those words had such an impact on me. In some way, we all have weaknesses, as well as old wounds we carry for a lifetime. In the church, we put out this image of having our lives so together, and we don't realize that we are broken just like everybody else. Instead of acknowledging our humanity, we fall into this trap of thinking we can abide all the rules and the regulations, we can fashion ourselves into perfect and complete human beings out of sheer willpower, out of sheer belief.

Peter thought he could. He told Jesus, "I will never deny you."

And Jesus said, "Oh, Peter."

We are just like Peter: we are going to fail. No matter how much of God we have in us, we are still going to make mistakes. We are going to mess up, and that's okay with God. Jesus came to identify not with our strengths, but with our weaknesses. The apostle Paul says, "It's not in my strength that I glory but in my weakness." And he said, "Of all sinners, I am chief."

Grace plays such a pivotal role.

This is a lesson I try to learn each day, and with my newfound devotion to the concept of grace, my attachment to traditional "salvation" has changed. I no longer believe that the ultimate goal is to get people to say to the sinner's prayer. We often get stuck on Jesus as a means to get to heaven rather than Jesus as a means of building heaven on earth. We act like people get saved and baptized and then they're done. They're in. They have to abide by the rules and attend the services, but mostly, we act like they've "got it."

Now more than ever, I see the flaws in this method, because it neglects the fact that our journey is long and eternal, and that at each step, grace will be with us. During this life, we will continually be challenged to grow deeper and closer to truth, and it's possible our learning curve will even continue after that.

In *Love Wins,* Rob Bell argues that death is not the final stroke. He points out that in the story of Lazarus and the rich man, the rich man calls out to Father Abraham after his death and asks if Lazarus can give him a drink of water—even after he has died! How Bell reads this is that God is still working with the rich man, still giving him a chance to understand, even after death.

The striking realization I came to is that God is doing this without me and my tireless efforts to "win" souls for him. After watching the world for a while you begin to think, *God's pretty big. He can connect with people anytime he wants to.*

Though it's a concept I sometimes struggle with, I still believe in that confusing, powerful thing called *sovereignty.* Something I learned when I was taking pilot's lessons is that you never go by what you feel when flying, because human beings are oriented to the ground. When I would close my eyes in an airplane, I always felt like I was turning right, but when I opened them we were level according to the horizon. That's a way I feel about my faith. Sometimes I don't feel like God's around. But somewhere deep within me, I know that God is at work in every life.

It makes me admire the churches that open the doors and say, "If you want to come, come. If not, God will meet you some other way." And the people who didn't follow the narrow, traditional path, or those who still haven't, or those of us who have fallen away, he will meet them at some other place.

To me, that's the message of Christ. After the resurrection, Jesus told Peter that he was going to be crucified upside down. And John was right next to Jesus. Peter asked, "Well, what about him?" Jesus said, "He is none of your concern. You follow me."

That's what the message is: for Dan Cox to follow Jesus. For you to follow Jesus. At some point, you have to start discovering who God is for you; you leave behind the faith practices that don't make sense, that don't feed you, and you search out and cling to those that do.

You move from the milk of the Word to the meat.

I truly believe that with the guidance of the Holy Spirit, people can navigate their own spiritual path, even in unconventional, unorthodox ways.

No, today I am not worried about saving people's souls, about their afterlife.

Instead, I am working on understanding Jesus and why he is so important for the present life. Because I know that if we really put into practice the core message of Jesus Christ, that message of loving-kindness and compassion and forgiveness, a lot of suffering will be relieved.

This message is not limited to any church or to any group of people or any culture. It's so much bigger than any of the traditional confines. And if individuals could really take up that mantle and live in the love of God the Father, emulating the sacrificial and loving commitment of the Son, with the guidance of the Holy

Spirit, they'd do more for the advancement of the kingdom than any institution ever could. They would be the nameless people who went about doing good, enacting change and healing in people's lives, making those small touches that are utterly transformative and transcendent.

And in my heart, I know that such a movement could bring about true salvation here in our midst.

And I pray that each of us will find that path that makes us whole.

ENDNOTES

1. Brian Kolodiejchk, *Mother Teresa, Come Be My Light: The Private Writings of the "Saint of Calcutta"* (New York: Doubleday, 2008), 186–7.
2. Matthew 11:3.
3. Diana Butler Bass, *Christianity After Religion: The End of Church and the Birth of a New Spiritual Awakening* (New York: HarperOne, 2012), 120.
4. Stephanie Cootnz, *Marriage, a History: How Love Conquered Marriage* (New York: Penguin, 2005), 5.
5. Ibid., 293.
6. Ibid., 310.
7. Geza Vermes, *Jesus in His Jewish Context* (Minneapolis, MN: Fortress Press, 2003), 11.
8. Ibid., 43.
9. Diana Butler Bass, *Christianity After Religion: The End of Church and the Birth of a New Spiritual Awakening* (New York: HarperOne, 2012), 46.
10. Ibid., 32.
11. Ibid., 161.
12. Ibid., 183.